THEY CALL ME
Mama Daktari

ANNE SPOERRY

Moulin

Moulin Publishing Limited
P.O. Box #560, Norval, Ontario, Canada L0P 1K0

Mama Daktari was written
with the collaboration of Claude Chebel,
translated by Madeleine Masson Rayner and
edited by Hugh de Glanville.

Canadian Cataloguing in Publication Data
Spoerry, Anne, 1918–
They call me Mama Daktari.

Translation of: On m'appelle Mama Daktari.
ISBN 0-9697079-9-1

1. Spoerry, Anne, 1918–
2. Physicians – Kenya – Biography.
3. Aeronoutics in medicine – Kenya.
4. Rural health services – Kenya. I. Title.
RA996.55.K4S6613 1996   610'.92   C96-900444-3

Cover photo by Andrea Booher
Design: Heidy Lawrance Associates
Printed and bound in Canada

In memory of
Sir Michael Wood, MB, BS, FRCS
—who inspired my life with AMREF

ACKNOWLEDGEMENTS

Thanks to
Madeleine Masson Rayner
for all her work on the translation,
and
Hugh de Glanville
for his editing.

Thanks to my family and colleagues at AMREF
for their help and support over the years.

CONTENTS

FOREWORD

The autobiography of Dr. Anne Spoerry traces two interrelated themes: the evolution of a remarkable organization, the African Medical and Research Foundation, serving isolated communities in East Africa; and the professional life of an incredible woman, Dr. Anne Spoerry, whose contributions have been equally remarkable throughout AMREF's four decades of existence.

AMREF began in 1957 as the Flying Doctor Service to serve seriously ill and disabled people who had no access to modern medical care in Kenya's remote communities. Its leaders soon recognized that important as the emergency and evacuation services by air were they did nothing to improve health care on the ground in these communities. Over the succeeding years AMREF has added visiting teams to provide basic health care and preventive measures such as: immunization in the communities; trained community health workers; assisted with water, sanitation and environmental health; engaged in research to assess and resolve local problems; and sponsored special programs to meet the needs, for example, in child and adolescent health and development and sexual and reproductive health. AMREF's geographic focus has spread from Kenya to Tanzania and more recently to other countries in East Africa, particularly those with domestic crises which threaten the health of massive numbers of displaced people as has been the case in Southern Sudan, Somalia and Rawanda. AMREF has now become a trusted partner with governments and with other non-governmental organizations in promoting health systems reform and forward looking policies. A consistent theme has been its advocacy for those most disadvantaged by poverty and geographic isolation.

The history of AMREF is rich in universal lessons for institutional leadership faced with the challenge of adapting policy and practices to the rapidly changing health scene. Dr. Spoerry's story traces the evolution of AMREF through the eyes of one of its most dedicated and colourful actors. Anne Spoerry, physician, aviator and adventurer, lost her heart to the people she has served in East Africa. Her life exemplifies the spirit that medicine knows no geographic frontiers.

John Evans, MD
Board of Directors
AMREF Canada

INTRODUCTION

Rarely in our lives are we fortunate enough to personally come across such a unique and exceptional individual as Dr. Anne Spoerry. For nearly 46 years in Africa, she has healed countless numbers of the sick, afforded hope to those in need, and provided inspiration and an example to those who work with her.

It is almost impossible to convey a true meaning of the Kiswahili term "mama daktari" in English. To appreciate its significance for an African, one must understand a cultural respect attributed to the combined qualities of age, wisdom, education, presence, and an ability to be useful to others. The best way to translate "mama daktari" is to actually describe Anne Spoerry— a dynamic, no-nonsense, medical doctor, nearly 80 years of age, piloting her own small single-engine aircraft, treating people in the most inaccessible and isolated areas of east Africa.

Today, the African Medical and Research Foundation (AMREF) is well known as a Nairobi based non-governmental health organization. It employs a staff of nearly 650 of whom 97% are African. Projects are implemented throughout the continent.

At its founding in 1957, however, AMREF was quite different. Then, nearly all of east Africa's population lived in rural areas. Hospitals and other health facilities were few and far between. The availability of doctors was even fewer. A small group of pioneering physicians living in Kenya and Tanzania realized that they could not wait for people to come to them. They had to go to where people lived.

Medical care had to be delivered in the bush—under a tree, in the back of a Land-Rover, or in a hastily arranged tent. The only way to reach isolated areas was by utilizing small aircrafts, often landing on poor or even nonexistent airstrips. For this purpose, AMREF's Flying Doctor Services were created.

Among her many remarkable achievements, Anne Spoerry was one of the first flying doctors. Now, almost 40 years later, she is the last of an original group. Her life experiences, both before and after coming to Africa, have been well worth documenting. The exceptional courage, the desire for adventure, and dedication to help those truly in need, becomes clearly evident in the following chapters.

I have been among those fortunate enough to have shared both a professional as well as personal relationship with Anne Spoerry. Because of these relationships, my life has been made richer. I am sure the same will be true for those who come to know her through the pages of this book.

Dr. Michael S. Gerber
Director General
AMREF
Nairobi, Kenya
May 1996

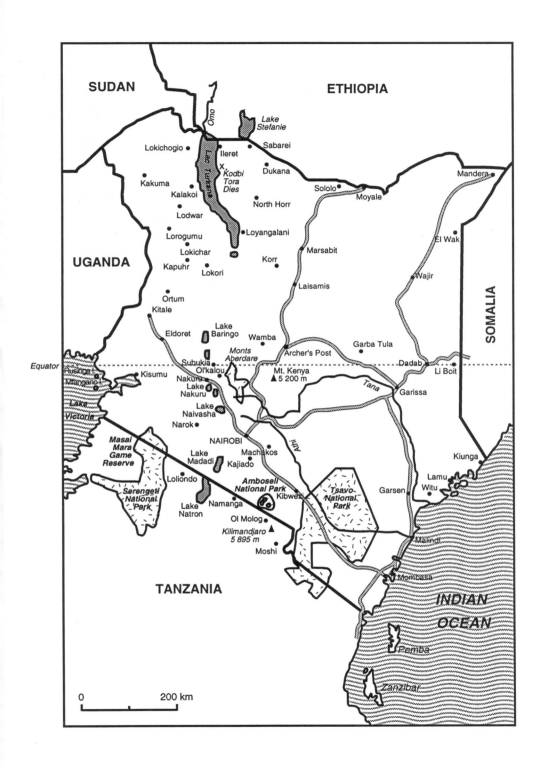

Chapter 1

CAMELS ON THE MOON

"Wilson, Alpha Zulu Tango, taxi clearance, please."

"Zulu Tango, taxi to holding point one-four."

It is 10 a.m. at Wilson Airport. The airfield reserved for light aircraft, is on Nairobi's southern boundary. Keeping to my usual five weeks' routine, I am waiting to take off for Marsabit, close to Kenya's northern border and the Ethiopian frontier.

For the last thirty years I've been taking health care and preventive medicine to basic outreach clinics in remote rural areas. My original brief was succinct in the extreme: "To establish a regular link, and to monitor the work of those staffing and running outreach clinics." In reality my mission was, and is, a great deal more complicated. Since 1964, I have been a flying doctor, attached to the service of AMREF—the African Medical and Research Foundation—which runs the flying doctor service and is funded, not by government, but by international agencies, private donors and our National offices in East Africa, Europe and North America.

I was born in 1918, and soon my plane will be twenty years old. We get along very well most of the time. It is a given that an aircraft is always in prime condition since it is regularly checked and serviced by experienced mechanics and vital parts are changed regularly, long before they show the slightest fault. Things are not quite so simple where the pilot is concerned, but my physical condition, like that of the plane, is strictly monitored by an annual examination carried out by a specialist. So as long as I am given the green light in the form of the priceless annual medical certificate, Zulu Tango and I will go on flying.

The AMREF offices are housed at the edge of the airport runway. To board my plane I only have to walk a few steps from my office, through the radio room to get my final instructions, then across to the apron. In the early days our office was a corrugated iron Nissen hut, which is still standing though now hemmed in by tall modern buildings.

In the beginning, our "fleet" consisted of only two planes, that of the founder of AMREF, the late Sir Michael Wood, and mine. Today we have a real fleet of eight machines, three of them twin-engined, flown by professional pilots, and have our own work and repair shops staffed by a team of highly trained mechanics.

It has been a long and amazing journey since those magical first days, and yet we are constantly aware that all our determined efforts count for little in the face of the immensity of the health problems this enchanting, ever-changing continent of Africa faces.

My own plane is a Piper Cherokee Lance PA-32, a single-engined aircraft equipped with a big, six-cylinder, 300 horsepower engine, and a retractable undercarriage. It is a fast and powerful machine, chosen specifically, not as an extravagant luxury, but for its impressive performance. A powerful engine is vital in Kenya, as even light aircraft have to fly at great heights. Nairobi is at an altitude of 5,500 feet and you have to climb steeply to 13,000 feet to get over prominent mountain crests. We always carry a full load of fuel. This is of the utmost importance, as we cover long distances with absolutely no possibilities of refuelling en route. Often we carry several people on board— patients, doctors, nurses and an occasional visiting journalist— as well as a cargo of medical supplies, spare radios and fresh vegetables from my garden. I have a little farm in the Rift Valley where I relax when I have time off from my medical safaris. Fresh produce is much appreciated by the medical staff living in desert clinics where they are deprived of fresh fruit and greens.

Our planes must also be able to climb steeply away from rudimentary grass or earth runways, of which few are longer than

500 or 600 yards, and contend with the excessive heat and the altitude. A really fast plane makes it possible to cover great distances and to make numerous stops in one day—a great bonus when the days on the Equator are so short. Speed is equally important when an urgent case has to be airlifted to hospital.

In the international alphabet, the registration number of my Cherokee is AZT (Alpha Zulu Tango), this makes some people smile, though the subject is hardly funny, since AZT is the abbreviation for a drug used to combat AIDS. Of course, my plane was registered long before that deadly illness made its appearance in the world, but there will always be people who see signs and portents everywhere.

"Zulu Tango, ready for take-off when cleared."

From the control tower comes the reply, "Zulu Tango cleared for take-off. Wind 120 at 12 knots."

Full throttle, and the Cherokee bounds forward. As soon as the airspeed indicator reaches 80, I lower the flaps to twenty degrees and the plane leaps into the air. This is the tried and tested technique of bush pilots. I use it even when I have plenty of runway—a pilot should always follow the same procedures. I once carried the Crown Prince of the Netherlands, himself a pilot, and he told me later that he couldn't get over my astonishing manoeuvres. He'd experienced nothing like them on his training course.

Hardly are my wheels up before I am already flying high above Nairobi's National Park, bordering Wilson Airport. That this nature reserve approaches so close to the city is extraordinary. From the skyscrapers of Nairobi one can look down at practically the whole range of African fauna. Dainty antelope gambol around giraffe; ostrich strut stiff-legged, keeping their distance from of a troop of baboons. A pride of lions, lying relaxed and peaceful in a clearing, are enjoying a morning nap. I often see rhinoceros quite near the runway—they seem to enjoy watching the planes flying in and out. Sometimes I take friends to the National Park to compensate for their disappointment at not seeing many wild animals on their safaris to the Amboseli or Mara game parks.

After a wide turn to the right, I head north. I switch from the Wilson frequency and call the AMREF radio operator to report that I am safely airborne, and that I'll call her on arrival at my destination. On my left are the Ngong Hills, so dear to Karen Blixen, better known to Western readers as Isak Dinesen; atop one of them is the grave of her friend Denys Finch-Hatton who, like me, loved to observe Africa from the air. Nearly every day I am privileged to fly over the incredible and beautiful landscapes seen in the film *Out of Africa*, based on Karen Blixen's book, and I never tire of looking down on the transformations brought about by the changing seasons. According to whether it is the dry or wet season, the lakes drain or overflow; the desert dries out and cracks, or blooms; rivers suddenly appear, while others dribble away into the sands.

I learned to fly late in life. I was forty-five, and I've never stopped trying to make up for lost time. I've already logged 8,000 hours' flying time, but when all is said and done, that only amounts to a total of 333 days.

North of Nairobi is a high plateau framed by the Aberdare mountains to the west and by Mount Kenya to the east, both covered by high-altitude forest. These highlands, the most fertile land in the country, are the source of many rivers, but their rushing torrents are soon dissipated once they reach the arid desert areas.

I pass over Nyeri, stronghold of the Kikuyu, Kenya's largest tribe. It was early this century that the British discovered and fell in love with this lush, fertile land, which reminded them of their beloved England. It was here, too, in the 1950s that they began to lose their paradise. At Nyeri there is a monument to the memory of those who fought in the war of independence, and in the revolt of the Mau Mau against the British colonists of the "White Highlands."

I was once a Girl Guide and I often spare a thought for Lord Baden-Powell, founder of the Scout and Girl Guide movement, as I fly over his last home, for it was here at Nyeri that he spent the final years of his life up to his death in January 1941.

I don't need to fly very high here as we are already at an altitude of 6,500 feet. I can clearly see the densely cultivated plantations of sisal, pineapple and coffee. The landscape, dotted with the round huts of the villages, reveals an enchanting palette of every shade of green, from the sombre, dark-green forest to the delicate, vernal green of the tea plantations.

Soon we will be close to massive Mount Kenya whose 16,500-foot peak may be visible but is more likely to be covered in the cloud mass that almost permanently enshrouds it. Very often we have to fly level with the cedar forests to avoid being caught up in the cloud layers. At this moment we are crossing the Equator, an event which never fails to astonish me, since at this latitude I am flying through scenery comparable to that of the Alps.

Sometimes we just cannot get through the clouds, so we have to make a right turn, and find another way through. The terrain below is chequered, and the weather patterns are localized, so that a little detour into the next valley can find everything changed and nature all smiles again. These are totally different flying conditions from those in Europe, where a whole country can remain sealed off for weeks at a time—at least when one flies as I do here, with no radio beacons and no flying "blind" on instruments.

Things move very fast on this leg of the journey. I took off barely an hour ago, and already the jigsaw of plantations and forests is receding into the background of my mind. I can now hardly see the great sombre mass of the Matthews range to the west. The arid, ridged terrain gives way to flat plains encrusted with spiky thorn bushes.

Shortly after leaving Isiolo, I see the turgid, muddy waters of Ewaso Ngiro, the last of the all-season rivers. Its banks are the last sanctuary of the flora and wildlife, the final refuge of zebra, giraffe and elephant, the ultimate mudbath for crocodile and hippo, before the arid, sun-scorched empty spaces in which the oxen seem to graze on sand, and the camels amble across a landscape that resembles the surface of the moon.

We now pick up the road to Marsabit, a thin, straight, scarcely visible track that has to be followed with the utmost care as it is the only landmark in this parched and barren wilderness, except for two rocks, one large, known as "The Cat," and a smaller one, "The Mouse." We are now in the "other" Kenya, a land of great plains and deserts, a completely different world unknown and unsuspected by tourists. For hundreds of miles lordly tribesmen lead their cattle, goats and camels to new pastures that may yield a few tufts of grass and perhaps a waterhole. Villages are few and far between; between them the barely discernible tracks are quickly erased. Sometimes we see the blistered surface of a small crater. Here and there, a few animals are gathered round *luggas*, dried-up river beds pitted with temporary wells, their banks covered with vegetation.

Under British colonial rule, and until 1970, this territory was the N.F.D.—the Northern Frontier District—access to which was strictly controlled, since neighbouring Somalia laid claim to it and conducted endless guerrilla campaigns in the hope of occupying it. After the Treaty of Arusha in 1967 relative peace prevailed for some twenty years, until the downfall of President Syad Barre of Somalia, when all hell broke loose and civil war in Somalia was ignited once more. Hordes of armed deserters became highway robbers known as *shiftas* and took refuge in north-east Kenya. In order to survive, they rustled flocks and attacked buses or trucks venturing onto the roads between Garissa and Wajir, and even as far west as Marsabit. This state of insecurity deeply affected Kenya, which already faced serious problems with refugees fleeing from its turbulent neighbours.

No matter what the disturbances in the desert regions of the north, it is always an adventure and a challenge to drive on the appalling, corrugated dirt tracks. There is no question that a plane is far superior to a car for the particular work I do, for it would have taken me days of misery and breakdowns to reach Laisamis, my next destination 200 miles from Nairobi.

I call Nairobi on the H.F. radio: "Foundation, Foundation, Zulu Tango in sight of Laisamis. Will call again when I have landed."

Flying low above the mission buildings framed by huts, I rev the engine up and down several times as a way of signalling my arrival and warning the herders to clear the makeshift runway of the livestock that like to congregate there. Skimming the ground to make sure all is safe, I touch down in a cloud of dust. It is a tight landing, as the runway is short, so I raise the flaps and brake as soon as the wheels touch.

A priest arrives at great speed in a Land-Rover. Like many of the northern mission stations, Laisamis is managed by Consolata, a Roman Catholic order. The good father seems to be in excellent spirits.

"Good news, Spoerry," he cries, beaming. "My road has been rebuilt, and I now have two windpumps, one for the church and the other for the hospital."

In these remote and underprivileged places it takes little enough to make people happy; yet only 200 miles away drivers caught in one of Nairobi's traffic jams are fuming with rage at the thought that they may be a few minutes late for an appointment in an air-conditioned office.

The hospital is a low building, with red and yellow walls, and a galvanized iron roof. It has forty-five beds, a simple operating theatre and a labour ward. In spite of the rudimentary equipment, the whole place is tidy, fresh and shining clean. There are three separate wards, one for men, one for women and the maternity ward. All are equipped with iron bedsteads painted blue. Both male and female patients have thoughtfully been provided with garments: *kikois* for the men and red gowns for the women, red being the traditional colour worn by the Samburu. This is Samburu territory. The Samburu are of Nilotic descent, akin to the Masai, speaking much the same language and sharing the same customs. Some of the patients are asleep, sheets pulled over their heads, a strange African custom that can be disconcerting to the uninitiated, who see motionless sheeted figures, resembling nothing so much as a ward full of corpses.

The Samburu who have drifted into Laisamis are not among those favoured by fortune. Much the greater part of their country lies to the south-west, in the more fertile regions around Maralal. The Government has been trying to teach them agricultural skills but it is no easy matter for them to renounce their traditional lifestyle. They have been used to raising cattle, which provide them with milk and blood, but they only eat the meat of their cattle at ritual ceremonies. Their staple diet consists of goat or mutton stew with soups made from roots and bark. More sociable than the Masai, the Samburu make it their business to be on good terms with their neighbours, but the authorities are hard put to it to persuade them to abandon some of their traditional customs. One that causes problems is their habit of regularly setting fire to the grasslands to make new grass grow green and tender. The fires often spread into the forests, which is not at all appreciated in a country continually struggling against deforestation.

The Samburu are an exceptionally handsome people. Tall and slender, they have fine, delicate features and long-lashed eyes. Their bearing is proud and dignified, and since they seldom complain, it is only in their eyes that one may read the story of their profound distress and sufferings.

The midday heat is suffocating, made bearable only by a faint current of air blowing through the paneless windows with their wire-mesh mosquito screens. Dr. James, the hospital physician, is a Zulu who has lived in Kenya for thirty years. He brings me those patients who he thinks have special problems. I examine a painfully emaciated youth covered with blueish blotches.

"He might have AIDS," ventures Dr James.

"He might certainly have contracted AIDS." The dread word, once hardly spoken aloud, is now commonplace in big urban centres in Kenya, with their continual flow of people—truck drivers, soldiers and prostitutes. All these make up a vicious circle, and nowadays AIDS has infiltrated even the remotest villages. "Let's have a blood test. I'll take a specimen back to Nairobi." There isn't the equipment to carry out HIV tests in these bush hospitals, and even if there were a miracle vaccine for AIDS, they could not afford to buy it.

Dr. James brings me another patient. He has tuberculosis (TB), and though he has been on chemotherapy for weeks, he is not responding. I make a note to have him transferred to a larger, better-equipped hospital where he can receive more sophisticated treatment. The next patient, a woman, has a painfully distended stomach, induced no doubt by a hydatid cyst, an extremely unpleasant ailment caused by a species of tapeworm. I explain this to Dr. James and recommend tests to determine whether my diagnosis is right. My last patient is a frail little girl, who looks at me with great sombre, unfathomable eyes.

My surgery being over, it is now time for me to tackle the radio. Knowing the radio at Laisamis was out of action, I have brought a spare. I get much amusement from telling people that I am a doctor, electrician, postman and breakdown-mechanic all rolled into one. In fact, there's a great deal of truth in my little jest. Bush doctoring doesn't take up all my time. Much of it is spent repairing broken-down radio sets. These are a constant headache. Almost from the start of AMREF, one of the founders' main objectives was to set up a network of two-way radio stations. Today, we have 145 high-frequency radio links, which are vital to the efficient functioning of the Foundation throughout Kenya and its neighbours, Somalia, Sudan, Tanzania and Uganda.

The bush clinics are mainly located in remote arid or semi-arid areas, and are not easily accessible by road. In spite of the great increase in motor traffic over the years, little has been done to improve the quality of the roads. Distances are vast, travelling is expensive and petrol stations are few and far between. This is where the plane, and its corollary, the radio, come into their own, providing the only link between the dedicated and isolated medical personnel and the outside world. By radio they can remain in permanent contact with our team in Nairobi. Besides being a great morale booster, permanent radio contact makes it possible to exchange information, confirm a diagnosis, order medical supplies or request immediate air transport for a sick patient. It is because the health of so many people depends on the proper functioning of the bush radios that I spend so much time servicing and repairing them on my rounds. This is why the radio is one of the most important patients to be examined when I arrive at a mission hospital, for the health of all patients depends on its fragile well-being.

During a quick break for lunch I meet with the rest of the hospital staff. They all speak English, albeit in an amusing hotchpotch of accents. Dr. James comes from South Africa; Sister Hildegarde, who heads the team, is German; the staff nurse is Italian. She is pretty and cheerful, and loves to tease me about the Foundation's financial problems, knowing how vulnerable I am in this particular respect, since I have to account for AMREFS' expenses. Money is a sore subject which nevertheless has to be tackled sooner or later. These missions exist on donations and have great difficulty in making ends meet. So do we, if on a somewhat larger scale, and this is why, when accounts have to be settled, I am absolutely inflexible. Charity begins with methodical and orderly accounts. All we ask of those in charge of the bush hospitals and clinics is that they should reimburse us for the medical supplies, vaccines and medical equipment bought on their behalf. My consultations are free, and there is no charge for the fuel consumed by my aircraft.

Our financial discussion is never unpleasant. I suspect that the good sisters make a special point of baiting me, to get a rise out of me, and to hear my Big Voice—the loud, booming tones I have zealously cultivated over the forty years I have lived in Africa. It is certainly an impressive voice, and it gets things done and people moving at a spanking pace. I know it is hardly a feminine accomplishment, but even women doctors have to develop strange resources to help them along.

At 3 p.m. my preparations for take-off from Laisamis produce a wild stampede among the hundred or so donkeys and goats. This second leg of my journey to Marsabit is just a hop. We fly fifty miles in twenty minutes over the Kaisut desert. The last of the circular *manyattas*, the Samburu villages, gives way to a terrain peppered with extinct volcanoes and volcanic craters called *gofs*. The monotonous countryside is relieved only by tongues of basalt. Though a threadbare cliché, "lunar" remains the best word to describe the landscape.

Yet people live here with their animals. They are the Rendille, who have absolutely nothing in common with their Samburu neighbours. Their origins are different—the Rendille come from Somalia, while the Samburu hail from the Nile Valley. The Samburu build their huts with branches and dried mud and abandon them when they migrate. The nomadic Rendille graze camels, and roam the deserts with their tents securely strapped to their beasts. Their tent-like homes are made of wooden frames covered with woven fibre and animal skins. Each camel walks forty miles a day and carries a load of up to 200 pounds. These herds of camel are indispensable to their owners, providing both transport and sustenance. The Rendille drink camel milk and blood tapped from the jugular vein.

As we fly out of Kaisut's inhospitable desert regions towards Marsabit, we catch sight of what seems either a miracle or a mirage: this is a vertical "oasis" formed by a volcano 5,500 feet high, against which clouds continually break, releasing their moisture as rain, so that an incredible variety of African flora flourish all the way down its steep slopes. Dense forest surrounds the *gofs*, the extinct craters filled with greenish water. The biggest is Paradise Lake. At one time I used to enjoy bathing there, until one of my friends contracted bilharzia—a disease transmitted by the baboons that haunt the area—from swimming in it.

The constant rainfall and abundant vegetation have turned Marsabit into a teeming wildlife reserve, a perfect paradise for zoologists. Created in 1900, the Marsabit National Park and reserve is the oldest of Kenya's national parks. The reserve benefits from the fact that, rising out of the desert like an island, it is difficult of access and well supervised, which discourages poachers; all these factors served to protect Ahmed, the famous elephant and star of the denizens of the forest, who was able to live in peace, prosper and grow to a ripe old age. He was a gigantic beast: his enormous tusks, each weighing 150 pounds, must have tantalized ivory poachers, then just starting to massacre the wildlife. The film director Christian Zuber, having encountered this venerable pachyderm, became anxious about Ahmed's future and began an energetic campaign to save him. Under Zuber's direction, an avalanche of postcards from all over the world landed on President Kenyatta's desk and he decided to make Ahmed a National Monument and to provide him with round-the-clock protection. In 1974 Ahmed died a natural death—in his own bed, so to speak. His skeleton and a plastic reproduction of the giant of the forest are now major attractions in the National Museum. In the forests of Marsabit, game rangers guard his successors by day and night.

From time to time I used to spend a few days in a lodge in the national park. From my window, through the mist, I could see the kudu, those gigantic striped antelope with their spiral horns, coming to drink at dusk. In the dry season lions drew very close, and when the rains came I watched baboons and buffalo disporting themselves. I remember, too, the deep wells in which the men stationed at each level passed buckets from hand to hand, singing in chorus all the while—whence the name, the "singing wells," given to their waterhole.

Curiously, Marsabit is not troubled by tribal squabbles. In times of drought all the northern tribes seek refuge here, forgetting petty differences and uniting in a "water truce." It is a sort of open town, neutral territory. The Turkana and the Somalis are the shopkeepers; the Samburu and the Boran cultivate the slopes; the Rendille and the Gabra sell their livestock in the marketplace. Imperative need shapes the laws and abolishes all ethnic barriers. This exceptional state of affairs offers hope to all who ponder the future of Kenya and the amalgamation of all its communities.

I begin my descent. The sky to the right is black, heralding a mighty storm over from the East. When it's not raining over Marsabit, you can be sure that rain is on the way. Landing here needs extreme caution. A few years ago, one of the mail planes crashed into the side of the mountain. The pilot had been told to fly low along a road leading to the airfield: he did so, but unfortunately he was following the wrong road. As soon as a hill or a mountain peak gets in the way of a mass of air, a tiny demon called the orographical wave makes its appearance. At high altitudes, the humidity turns into instant rain—something pilots need to remember, even on the Equator. Fortunately, Marsabit's airfield has a fairly rain-resistant tarmac runway, and it is possible to land between downpours.

Just as I touch down the heavens open, and I am trapped in the cabin of the plane for a good hour. The hospital staff who have come to meet me and fetch their medical supplies have to sit out the deluge in their car.

As a rule, I don't visit patients in the government-run Marsabit Hospital, which has its own medical staff. We are called in to help only with serious operations or to airlift out critical cases. Today, thank goodness, there are no emergencies.

A police jeep filled with jerricans of fuel charges through the last drops of rain. It is important to top up the fuel in the plane and to take extra reserves on board since for the next few days I will be flying to places where fuel will be unavailable. I dash out of the plane to supervise the tanks refuelling. The fuel inlet is on the rain-drenched wing and it is vital to prevent any rainwater getting into the fuel, for this would make a breakdown in the bush certain, raising the possibility of being marooned in a total wilderness. As I don't want to make the young, rather clumsy soldiers nervous, I hide my impatience, but I am seriously worried by the time they are taking. In less than two hours, night will have fallen, and before that I must reach my next port of call, Sololo, on the Ethiopian border.

At 5 p.m. I take off, flying north over the desert and the long, thin shadows of the thorn bushes. Forty minutes later I touch down at Sololo. This smooth, grassy landing strip is unusually luxurious and well-kept for a small village hidden away in the foothills of the great Ethiopian mountain ranges. That it is maintained in such superb condition is due entirely to the efforts of the police who man the post here in order to keep watch on the frontier, abuzz with experienced and ruthless cattle-raiders, cattle-rustling being a sport much practised in this region, which is peopled by the Boran, who are both shepherds and farmers.

It's high time to land. Night is falling when the reception committee, composed of the young lads of the village, surrounds my plane. They always arrive at the rendezvous on the dot, though their punctuality has nothing to do with their health—they have come to collect the supply of newspapers and other reading matter that I bring them regularly. They read English and are avid for knowledge of what is happening in the great world outside. It doesn't matter to them that the papers are several weeks old; the mere fact of reading them makes these youngsters feel that they are keeping in touch. It is for these boys and others like them that I buy newspapers and magazines. I have no qualms about importuning my friends to let me have their discarded reading matter, and it is no secret that I "confiscate" any stray papers and magazines I come across.

I arrive at the clinic, which is attached to the Catholic mission, to be greeted by a young married couple. Silvio is an orthopedic surgeon who was stationed here when he did his military service in the Peace Corps. Nostalgia for his great adventure then later drew him back, and he returned with his wife, Teresa, who specializes in diabetes, and their young son.

During supper, enriched by my contribution of wine and fresh vegetables, neither of which have graced the table for some time, Silvio, sure of a sympathetic ear, pours out his problems. They are many. His 100-bed hospital has an operating theatre, but visits from anesthetists and plastic surgeons are few and far between, and his operating theatre could be used more.

"This part of the world," says Silvio, "is no bed of roses, and life for the Boran is tough. Not only do the cattle-rustlers steal their cattle, but they leave a trail of casualties behind them. Some of them have severe gunshot wounds, while many of the young boys have been castrated."

The government hospital at Moyale, the neighbouring town, is run-down and scarcely functioning so that nearly all the sick, including Ethiopian refugees, come to the mission hospital at Sololo. Recently, forty refugee children died of measles, and since then the mothers have brought their children to the clinic to be immunized. Fortunately, I have brought Silvio a big batch of vaccine.

Next morning, I arrive at the hospital as dawn is breaking over the magnificent backdrop of the towering mountain ranges. I accompany Silvio on his round and he points out several children suffering from Pott's disease—spinal tuberculosis. In this condition the vertebrae collapse and press on the spinal cord, so that the children can no longer walk. It is a pitiful sight to see those helpless little ones, limp as rag dolls.

Chemotherapy for tuberculosis is efficacious but must be started in the very early stages of the disease, and the patients often need an operation. This illness should be eradicated as soon as we are able to vaccinate all the children with BCG. But how, and when will that be? Only when the mothers, convinced at last that our treatment is successful, come down from the mountains or cross the deserts to get to the clinics. One can only hope that Silvio will still be around when this miracle happens.

We continue on our round. Silvio says, "Just look at all those children suffering from burns. I tell you again, Anne, we urgently need a plastic surgeon."

I know he is right. These children, and others like them, are used to sleeping close to open fires and boiling pots. Every day I am confronted with shrivelled little limbs and small, horribly scarred faces. It is partly to combat this disastrous problem that AMREF was founded thirty-five years ago by three specialists in plastic and reconstructive surgery, and these doctors laid their resources, reputations and professional skills on the line to operate on and repair the hideously damaged faces of these little victims.

Silvio takes me aside and whispers, "What do you think is the matter with this lad? He looks like a case of AIDS to me."

I look down at the emaciated, peaked adolescent, with the long-lashed eyes of a sick deer. His knees are badly discoloured. "That's one more blood sample to take back to Nairobi."

Silvio says passionately, "We simply must have the means to make the necessary tests here, Anne. Waiting for them to be done in Nairobi takes far too long."

At 10 a.m. I leave Sololo, delighted and moved by the dedication and enthusiasm shown by Silvio and Teresa. I am sure they will eventually get the help they need to make the changes they know are necessary for the welfare of their patients. I am also certain that their energy will not dribble away into the sands, that their devotion to their work will not melt in the sun. As the years go by, they are not likely to give way to the fatalism and discouragement I have so often seen in those who live and work in Africa.

Flying due west, I follow the big white markers along the frontier and reach Dukana half an hour later. In order to get straight
to my destination, I've had to enter Ethiopian air space, flying
over brown hills with no sign of life. I know I am technically in
the wrong, but to whom should I apply to get permission to over-
fly this territory? As far as I can see there's not a living soul down
there.

On the outskirts of Dukana, I again find *manyattas*—the village huts arranged in a circular pattern. The inhabitants of this
part of the country are the Gabra. They are Couchites, related to
the Boran and, like them, camel breeders. Their sacred mountain, the Furole, is one of my larger landmarks in a place that has
few. Don't try to find Dukana in a guide book. It is never mentioned, for there is absolutely no reason for anyone, with the
exception of doctors and the police, to come here. Even the
Boran did not choose to live here, but they were driven out of
Ethiopia in the last century.

The red-earth airstrip is covered with camels. My low-level
pass spreads panic amongst the herd and I have to circle several
times before the herders have cleared the runway and re-estab-
lished order. Dukana is really no different from any other arid
area I visit. There are wells around which the herds gather, a
church or mosque, and then the school. Any health facility is
always an afterthought. Dukana's new, government-funded dispensary is nearing completion. The nurses' living quarters are
still unfinished, because the contractor did a runner with the
funds allocated for this project. His felony raises a good laugh
among the inhabitants—while theft from individuals is cruelly
and severely punished, stealing from the amorphous State, is
warmly applauded. This raises an interesting point: do we
Westerners have the right to pontificate on this particular question of principle and morality?

To be frank, nothing works in Dukana, certainly not the
radio. I begin by tackling this problem. First of all I discover
that the battery is flat. After a great deal of haggling, I manage
to borrow one from the police, at the same time begging them
to recharge the old battery. Their efforts are a total failure. It is

impossible to contact Nairobi. I finally discover that the outside aerial is at an impossible angle. I make it known, loudly and in no uncertain terms, that I have no intention of leaving until the radio has been fixed and is again in perfect working order. To make up for having disturbed their peaceful existence, I later hold a clinic especially for the police. There's little wrong with them, apart from a few gastric upsets, as these young policemen are very well nourished.

As a general rule, I prefer to examine patients on the runway, in the shelter and shade provided by the plane. Among them are some who are really ill, who have walked countless miles with their flock or herd to get to my clinic. Dealing with them is hard work, for these are classic cases of tuberculosis, malaria or huge hydatid cysts. To these ills are added snakebites and wounds caused by wild animals. Two years ago I watched a cloud of dust blowing my way. From it emerged a group of Gabra carrying two men mauled by lions who had attacked their herds. One was in a very bad way and I rushed him to hospital at Sololo; the second man was strapped to a camel and taken to the clinic in North Horr. Six months later, in the same place, I treated two other men mangled by a lion in exactly the same way.

At noon, under a blistering sun, I get back to my plane and take off for Sabarei, a frontier observation post. It only takes a quarter of an hour to fly there. I can see a few blockhouses near the runway, some spindly bushes, and in the distance, the rugged mountains. Being posted here could hardly be called promotion. An inscription in the soldiers' quarters neatly sums up the ambience of the place: "Only a Sabarean knows what loneliness is."

I stay just long enough to take on board a soldier who has to get to Ileret, twenty minutes' flying time away. The landscape does not improve. We fly over a salt desert, the Chew Bahir lake, which resembles the "chotts" (salt marshes) of North Africa, before making a bumpy landing on a sand strip peppered with the hollowed-out nests of carmine bee-eaters. Far below the runway is Lake Turkana (formerly Lake Rudolph), also known as the Jade Sea. Misted over by a heat haze, it stretches further than the eye can see. The first time I came to Ileret I remember thinking that this is how our planet would look after a nuclear war. Blocks of lava, petrified trees, great stretches of pallid water and misshapen bushes continually blasted by fierce winds, an inferno under an empty sky; in short, this would be the perfect setting for a science fiction film depicting the end of the world. The actors would have to be hordes of starving, desperate people in rags, fighting one another for a crust or a bone. However, I soon realized that I was wrong. Pessimism plays no part in the African makeup, and the banks of Lake Turkana are not the end of the world, but its beginning.

I am proud to number two outstanding men as friends, archaeologists Yves Coppens and Richard Leakey, who, twenty-seven years ago, began excavations in this region and proved without a shadow of a doubt that here, and only here, was the cradle of mankind. Each time I pass through Ileret, I remember the summers I spent with Yves Coppens's team on the banks of the Omo, a short distance to the north.

The first time was in 1969, just as Neil Armstrong was setting foot on the moon. By spending billions of dollars, boffins had finally succeeded in putting a man on another heavenly body. At the same time, at a tiny fraction of the cost, in a remote corner of Africa, scholars scratching through the African soil were quietly, without any fanfare, uncovering the mystery of our origins. Which of these men, one wonders, took the greatest step forward for mankind?

From Koobi Fora, some miles to the south, is where Leakey directed operations, he described the surrounding countryside as he envisioned it might have been two million years ago.

"Imagine," he wrote, "spreading out from the banks of the lake are acres of grasslands, and groves of trees among whose branches swing mischievous monkeys. Elephants, or at least their ancestors, feed peacefully on leaves and branches. Their trunks are smaller, their tusks are shorter, and thicker [than today]. Nearby, a group of men are enjoying a chat. They are small but they stand straight on their two legs. Their massive foreheads are low. Close at hand, a group of workmen are cutting into stones, from which they will fashion tools. The sky is blue and clear, fresh streams chuckle through the prairies."

Leakey animated his vision by having a disturbing diorama constructed for the Nairobi Museum. African visitors spend a long time gazing at it. It affects them in different ways: some laugh, while others remain plunged in thought. Those whose families still live in the same bush as shown in the model must reflect that in two million years life hasn't changed all that much. I am sure that most of those who stand gazing silently at Leakey's reconstruction feel a legitimate pride in their past. Is Africa not the mother of us all, and do the Africans not have every right to respect and be proud of their ancestors? Perhaps the most astonishing feat of all is the way the paleontologists have managed to evoke such precise and detailed images of the past from a few bones, clumsily fashioned stones and fossilized spores.

The tribe who lives around Lake Turkana are far from primitive. Theirs is a very structured society, and they have developed the art of survival to an astonishing degree. The trouble is that this is the main meeting point of a number of other tribes of various origins and cultures, some of whom are extremely hostile. Added to their traditional rivalries are the persistent echoes of the warfare that for decades has riven Ethiopia, the Sudan and Somalia. Banditry is thinly disguised as guerrilla warfare, which today is infinitely more murderous and deadly than it was, the spears and daggers of yesteryear replaced by the deadly Kalashnikovs that are now so easily obtainable.

Today, a nasty surprise awaits me at Ileret. The mission is two and a half miles from the landing strip, and the bad news is brought to me from the mission by foot-messengers who tell me that the only available vehicle has had a breakdown. I firmly refuse to walk to the mission at two o'clock under a blazing sun. So I set up my clinic in the shade of the plane and await the days events.

I don't have long to wait for the patients to find me. Most of them were already in the vicinity. As in every village I visit, everyone knows my schedule and habits. This is why I keep to regular appointments during each five-week circuit not the first, fifteenth, or twenty-fifth of the month, dates that would make no sense to these people, for whom time is measured solely by the phases of the moon.

As I am expected to help out with public relations duties when necessary, I look after the journalists who sometimes accompany me on my visits. I know they never fail to be amused by my working uniform, which consists of old jeans, patched boots and a bush shirt, the whole finished off with a baseball cap. So far as I can see it is a sensible outfit. I would look pretty silly piloting my plane in a Chanel suit with high-heeled shoes, or in a white coat and matching surgeon's cap.

One item of my equipment that seems to astonish the press people is the big Swiss Army knife I always carry, not to defend myself against attack, but for its many practical uses. I use the big blade to open boxes, dismantle radios, cut pills in half or as an invaluable aid at mealtimes. When I share the frugal fare so generously offered at the missions, the best silver is not usually brought out for me.

Most journalists have vivid imaginations, and can be "economical with the truth." They love what they call a good human story, which is how the legends of the uses to which I put my Swiss Army knife were born. I am supposed to use the various blades to carry out operations, lance abscesses and boils—and goodness knows what other fantastic anecdotes are spread around. These reporters don't know that surgeons and doctors the world over abide strictly by very precise rules, that we use only properly sterilized surgical instruments. These stories irritate me. They may look impressive in a magazine, but I'm not sure it pleases our generous donors when they read of a doctor operating on patients with a penknife sterilized in the flame of a cigarette lighter.

For once at Ileret I do not have to treat any serious cases. My patients amble off with their little supplies of tablets, and I begin to think of striking camp. At this moment, however, an old man in tattered rags suddenly appears. He is a shepherd, and he leans on his tall cane, clasping to his chest his only other worldly possession, a carved head-rest that also serves as a stool. He is emaciated and weak, though he has probably walked a long way to reach me.

The people of Ileret do not seem to know him. Probably he does not belong to the local tribe; perhaps he comes from Ethiopia. As he hardly speaks and does not understand Swahili it is difficult to communicate with him. It's obvious that he is very ill, and is unable to eat because of the enormous neck glands caused either by cancer or tuberculosis.

I come to an instant decision. I will take him with me, hoping to find a hospital on the way that will care for him. Since I don't know his name I called him Old Fellow. I'm certain he has never been in a plane in his life, but he doesn't seem in the least nervous of becoming my passenger. When we hoist him aboard, his wasted frame is as light as a child's, and he is so thin that the seat belt barely holds him in place. Thinking he may well be airsick, I hand him a plastic bag, explaining in mime how to use it. A short while after take-off, which doesn't seem to upset him in the least, he taps my shoulder. I assume he is going to vomit, but all he wants is my permission to stretch out on my bags on the next seat.

Our next port of call is North Horr, a forty-five-minute flight to the south-east. This relatively large centre has an excellent hospital which I hoped will take in my protégé. Old Fellow, who is probably no more than fifty, has a very engaging personality. In spite of looking so unwell, he has wonderfully fine, clean-cut features, like all Nilotics, and his movements are graceful, even elegant. He quickly fathoms how to get out of the plane over the wing, something most normal, healthy Westerners find difficult to cope with.

North Horr is a far more pleasant place than Ileret for it has the benefit of vegetation in the shape of the little doum palm trees. The staff of the mission have taught the local inhabitants to make basketware that is very popular, and sells well, even as far afield as Nairobi. North Horr is also famous for its enormous herds of camels. Indeed, camels are so thick on the ground that I can hardly see the runway.

I am met by a couple of male nurses in a brand-new Land-Rover, a gift of the United Nations, who have mounted a campaign to fight AIDS, in the area as evidenced by the logo on the doors of the shiny new vehicle. In fact, AIDS is not the major problem here, but international organizations have their own ideas of what is of most importance, and one should never look a gift horse in the mouth.

When I ask Sister Brigitte, who is in charge of the hospital, to take in my old shepherd, she flings her arms in the air. "It's impossible," she cries. "My hospital is full to bursting, and on top of everything else I am trying to cope with a malaria epidemic."

She has a point. The hospital is so full that men and women are being forced to share the same wards; most of them are on drips; and, because of the shortage of beds, some of the patients have to lie on the floor. In one corner a young girl lying down, her naked breasts hastily covered with a towel. Her face, in its frame of lustrous dark hair, is one of the most beautiful I have ever seen. This is what the Queen of Sheba must have looked like. When she turns her gaze on me, her great golden eyes are bright with fever.

After I have fought Sister Brigitte with every argument in the book, we eventually come to a satisfactory, if temporary, arrangement for Old Fellow. His most urgent needs are to be fed and rehydrated, so he will be put on a drip during the night, and tomorrow I'll fetch him and try to find him another refuge where he can be cared for. (Though she has agreed to take him in, Sister Brigitte remarks reasonably enough that the locals are Gabras and that my shepherd is in all probability a Geluba—belonging to a different tribe is a matter of great importance in a country hospital, for it can lead to disruption in the wards.)

It is four o'clock. There won't be any lunch for me today. I snatch a little time off to share a cup of tea with Sister Brigitte and her team, which includes an adorable little girl who follows them about like Mary's Little Lamb. While looking after her parents' flock in the desert, she was bitten by a viper. The mission saved her life and adopted her. I expect one day she will become a nurse.

The police mounted on camel-back make it their business to clear the runway of beasts that have once again occupied it. I take off and fly south-west, and in a quarter of an hour I am back at Lake Turkana, only this time I'm at its southern end, which is no greener than the north, except at Loyangalani, an oasis that will be my last port of call today. A few minutes before landing, I fly over the territory of the El Molo, a small tribe of fishermen. This is one of the oddest and most eccentric tribes in Kenya. Their very existence is a mystery, and their survival a matter for amazement. Their name, which means "poor devils," was given them by neighbouring tribes who despised their peaceful lifestyle and had no scruples about kidnapping their womenfolk. The birth rate of the El Molo is low and inbreeding has led to degeneration. The El Molo are a fossil people, like Richard Leakey's primitive man. There are only a few hundred of them left, and their genes will probably be absorbed by those of the more powerful and resistant Samburu or Turkana.

From the shelter of their palm-leaf huts, the fossil folk have spotted my plane, and, for sure, they will be waiting for me at the mission hospital. I know them well. Their main problems stem from deformities of the bones and curvature of arms and legs due to high concentrations of fluorine in the lake water.

From time immemorial, the El Molo earned their living by fishing Lake Turkana using frail but perfectly adapted rafts made from doum palm trunks. Then one day an officious civil servant had the bright idea of releasing public funds to give the El Molo a plastic motorboat. The local fishermen, unused to working with modern machinery, were relieved when the Government produced a Luo captain who hailed from Lake Victoria and was paid the same fat salary as a skipper in Mombasa. The El Molo abandoned the motorboat to the captain and continued to use their traditional craft, leaving the wily skipper to charter the boat to tourists. This freshwater mariner loved uniforms, and never missed an opportunity to decorate his bush shirt by scrounging spare chevrons from the professional pilots who touched down at Loyangalani. He proudly displayed three or four stripes, according to the rank of the latest donor.

Eventually, the motorboat suffered a permanent breakdown. For a long time it floated at its mooring, while the captain kept his post and continued to receive his salary and to strut around the bar of Oasis Lodge, until the funds allocated for this particular whimsical project finally ran out.

After such a tough day I am glad of the haven offered by Loyangalani. I wash off the dust of the desert in the mission's swimming pool. Yes, they have a pool, a large one, in which one can actually swim. It is filled from a volcanic source with water coming out at 40°C; an Italian millionaire who was in love with the place gave the pool to the mission. At nightfall, a strong wind whistles through the greenery, the tree ferns and the *mswaki* bushes, whose twigs the Africans use to clean their teeth. The dramatic effect of the winds is heightened by the chirring of the nightjars and the noisy beating of their wings.

Father Francis, head of the mission, who comes from Colombia, has a great sense of humour and collects straw hats. His colleague, Father Mario, is a dedicated mechanic, a useful hobby here where there is always something in need of repair, whether it be a Land-Rover or a broken-down generator. Maintaining the electricity supply is a continual worry. The diesel generators function for only a few hours at night to economize on both fuel and plant. If you ask Father Mario why he doesn't harness the wind, he gives you a wry smile and escorts you to the back of the building to show you what appears to be a pile of kindling, but which is in fact all that remains of the toughest and finest wind pumps available on the world market.

Loyangalani, must bear the brunt of the crazy, gale-force winds that tear down from Mount Kulal. Even at night there is no respite from the torrid gusts, which make sleep difficult.

After lights-out I visit Oasis Lodge, the Mecca, if one may so call it, of a modest tourist trade. Wolfgang, the German owner of the lodge, is a flamboyant character. He freely admits that he never takes precautions against malaria. "I drink far too much whisky for the mosquitoes to dare to bite me," he says. His main subject of conversation centres around the *shiftas*—those bands of roving brigands whose sporadic appearances and raids do little to encourage the spread of tourism around here. "Lodges" in East Africa are a kind of inn, usually found on established tourist site. The word is difficult to translate accurately, but its nearest approximation would be a holiday village complex. A lodge has a main building, complete with bar, restaurant and swimming pool. Surrounding the main block are "bandas"—individual well-appointed cabins.

Oasis Lodge is haunted by the memory of the tragic events that took place here in 1965. I had just ended my first year of work with the flying doctors, and at that time armed bands of guerrillas were creating havoc by harrying all those who came within their reach. They were backed and equipped by the Somalis who, since Independence, had claimed this territory on the pretext that its population had the same ethnic roots and spoke the same language as they did. The national emblem of Somalia is a star whose fifth point is supposed to represent Northern Kenya. The demands of the Somalis made a mockery of the sacrosanct principle of preserving the frontiers inherited from the colonial regime, and Kenya, refusing to be blackmailed, stood firm against the intruders. The skirmishes degenerated into a real war. The *shiftas* took to raiding villages. Access to the northern district was restricted, and I had to visit my hospitals under military escort. Although the Treaty of Arusha officially ended hostilities, so vast was the territory in which the *shiftas* operated, and so adept were they at vanishing into thin air, that these heavily armed marauding bands continued to ravage the countryside.

Oasis Lodge was then owned by a couple called Sorsby, who from the beginning had generously helped to fund the fledgling AMREF. Before Independence, Sir Malin Sorsby had been the director of East African Airways. His first wife had died in a plane accident when the aircraft in which she was travelling crashed on top of Mount Kilimanjaro. It was not until ten years later that climbers found the debris of the plane and the frozen remains of the victims.

Before the Loyangalani tragedy, Lady Sorsby, Sir Malin's second wife, had recognized the immense potential of tourism in Kenya and had already created two lodges, one at Samburu and the other at Maralal. She had taken on Guy Poole, an ex-Maltese sailor, to manage Loyangalani. All the resources for building a lodge were already on the site she had chosen. There were a few thatched buildings and a small swimming pool, built in 1959 by members of a University of California scientific expedition that had spent six months here, studying the geology, botany and fauna of Lake Turkana.

Guy Poole was the ideal choice for the job of manager of a lodge. Energetic and resourceful, he could turn his hand to anything. He owned a powerful boat, *Lady of the Lake*, in which he sometimes took me fishing. He had built a fence around the lodge and planted a pretty flower garden. The fence did not, however, deter the local goats and donkeys from getting into the garden and grazing happily on the lawns and flower beds. Incensed by their ravages, Guy Poole, would rush outside, firing shots into the air to frighten the intruders away. Once he confiscated a donkey that refused to leave. So far as the local Rendille and Samburu shepherds were concerned, these were heinous offences, and Guy was far from popular with them. He was, however, on good terms with the El Molo fishermen, whom he helped as much as he could.

It was at this juncture that the government had the bright idea of developing Loyangalani by building a mission, a school and a fishing co-operative. In no time at all a fully fledged commission was established and white surveyors spent their time busily lining up suitable sites. The sight of all these strangers led the local inhabitants to fear that there were plans to take away their water and chase them out of Loyangalani. Since the bureaucrats, in their usual high-handed way, had not seen fit to consult the African locals or to explain any of the plans and improvements that were being studied, suspicion and fear among the locals reached a boiling point. Their hatred became fixed on Oasis Lodge and Guy Poole, whom they held responsible for all the evils they expected to befall them. The mutterings rose to a crescendo, and the *shiftas*, well known to the locals, were invited to stop Guy Poole from interfering in their lives.

One Friday morning, a few days before Christmas, I met Guy

Poole and his wife Lilian near the New Stanley Hotel. They were doing their Christmas shopping. We had a brief chat during which they told me they were going to call on Michael Wood, head of AMREF, whose office at that time was in the town centre. After that, Guy said he intended to return to Oasis Lodge, while Lilian and the children, who were at school, would remain in Nairobi.

The next evening, back on my farm in Subukia, I was listening to the messages on the radio security network that linked the local farmer to the outside, when I heard that an attack had taken place at Loyangalani and that several people had been killed. Since Loyangalani had no means of communication with the outside, a man had travelled the forty-five miles to South Horr with the terrible news. On that fatal Friday afternoon, Guy Poole had flown back to the lodge. The pilot who had flown him from Nairobi was anxious to get back, as there were only two hours left before nightfall. Hastily downing his glass of beer, he said, "If anyone wants to fly back with me we're leaving in a minute." A young man, the nephew of the Italian building contractor who was enlarging the swimming pool, jumped at the offer of a free flight and rushed off to change, a snap decision that saved his life.

Once the plane had gone, the only people left in the lodge were Guy Poole, an old Italian who drove the truck used to carry supplies, and the African staff. Since the construction work was in progress the lodge was closed to guests. Towards evening, Father Stallone, a Catholic priest who was supervising the building of his mission close by, dropped in for a chat and a drink. At approximately seven o'clock, the three men heard the sounds of shots and screams. Guy Poole gave one of the servants the key to the gun cupboard and told him to bring back some rifles at the double. Poole would have been better advised to go on this vital errand himself, for the man did not return, even supposing he ever had any intention of doing so.

Guy, the priest and the old driver were hustled off to one of the cabins where they were tied to chairs with electric flex. A guard was left standing over them, while the other *shiftas* went on a wild rampage. They ransacked the lodge, keeping up an indiscriminate barrage of gunfire. Having drained the bar dry, they returned to the cabin in which Guy and his friends were being held prisoner, and there they murdered two of their victims, shooting them in the back as they sat tied to the chairs. Having wrecked all the other cars, the bandits then forced the old driver at gunpoint to help them load their loot into the Land-Rover. They then drove away. After twenty miles the vehicle ran out of petrol and the bandits fled into the night, taking the driver with them. He was never seen again.

Billy Bunford, then administrator of AMREF, called me on the radio and asked me, since I was the nearest to the scene, to get there as soon as I could. At dawn on Sunday I loaded my plane with first-aid boxes. Nobody knew for sure what had happened and I thought perhaps I might have to look after the wounded. Already the cloud hung so thickly over the mountains that I had to fly to Loyangalani via the Rift Valley. There I found a police plane bringing Lady Sorsby to Oasis Lodge. The two corpses had been placed in body bags: there was nothing anyone could do for them.

My old friend "Punch" Bearcroft, head of the Flying Police Squad, was in charge of the investigation. His nickname came from his amazing facial resemblance to that much-loved puppet. Having lost a hand in a tractor accident, he had retaken his pilot's licence with a hook for a right hand. He started the Kenya Police Reserve Airwing during the Emergency, and after Independence he stayed on to command it. Despite his handicap, he could fly any aircraft, including the DC3, and when helicopters were added to his fleet he learned to fly them as well, determined to remain on a par with his officers.

The tragedy at Oasis Lodge affected everyone, particularly those who had known the victims, who were doing their best to improve conditions in this underprivileged place. I was angry with the El Molo, who were, I knew, well aware of the plotting that had taken place before the murders. They had disappeared without warning, even though they had every reason to be grateful to Guy Poole. He had asked them to organize performances of their traditional dances for the tourists. In exchange for a dance they were given enough mealie-meal flour to feed their community for at least a month.

Sick at heart, Lady Sorsby closed the lodge, and put it on the market. The El Molo were shocked and upset. "Don't you dare come and complain to me," I said sharply, having listened to their lamentations. "You knew exactly what was going to happen, so why didn't you warn Mr. Poole? He was very good to you. You could have saved his life."

"It was written. It was the fault of the good God," they said dolefully. They did not want to admit that, by warning Guy Poole, they would have laid themselves open to reprisals from the Rendille, who most certainly were party to the murders. The only good thing to come out of this terrible drama was that a permanent police station was installed at Loyangalani. The lodge was sold and reopened to tourists. I often spent the night in Banda 6, the scene of the crime—I don't believe in ghosts.

Morning surgery today at the Loyangalani clinic is easy. There are no serious cases, though there are some spectacular white blotches on brown skins due to athlete's foot, the result of paddling in water at a temperature of 50°C in the shade—only there isn't any shade.

I must now deal with a Turkana family. The homeland of this tribe is really west of Lake Turkana, but their influence stretches as far afield as Loyangalani. They share the same Nilotic roots as the Samburu and the Masai, but their culture is less rigid, and their resources more varied. Nomadic herders, they graze a variety of beasts, from camels to cattle, donkeys and goats. They are adaptable and can turn their skills to farming or fishing. They do not practise circumcision or excision, replacing these customs by the extraction of the lower incisor teeth.

Unlike other tribes, the Turkana do not treat their womenfolk as inferior beings, which is probably why this family has come to consult me about one of their daughters, who has recently developed a pronounced limp. It doesn't take long to discover the cause: the poor child probably tripped over some stones while carrying a heavy load, dislocating her femur as she fell. As she did not mention the accident or complain, her parents only knew that she had started to limp. A permanent limp is a tremendous handicap among people who spend most of their lives walking, in a community in which the infirm and crippled are rejected as useless dead-weights. I now have to tackle the father. He does not speak Swahili, so a nurse translates my diagnosis and the treatment I suggest.

"Tell him his daughter can certainly be cured and she will walk normally again. But, to bring this about, she will have to go to the hospital in Wamba, where she will have to stay in bed with a weight attached to her leg so it can be put straight. This treatment may last some weeks, and will cost you 700 shillings."

The family then move away to discuss the matter. The father comes back to tell me he wants his daughter to have the treatment I have prescribed. I thought as much, for in spite of their simple garments the Turkana are far from poor. All the father has to do to raise the necessary cash is to sell one of his flock. In Africa, appearances are misleading and this goes for both man and nature.

Leaving Loyangalani at nine in the morning I catch a glimpse of South Island, a cone of lava inhabited by goats. Lake Turkana, an inland sea a hundred and fifty miles long, is far richer in wildlife than one might imagine. Two of the other islands are home to enormous crocodiles and a port of call for thousands of migratory birds. It seems that long ago, in the distant past, the lake was linked to the Nile, since the aquatic fauna of the two bodies of water are very similar. Besides crocodile and hippo, there are giant Nile perches weighing up to about 300 pounds. These and tilapia form part of the staple diet of those living on the lake shores, as well as providing great sport for the tourists who come to fish these waters—sport that carries an element of danger, as the Jade Sea is often the scene of sudden, violent storms. Visitors should heed the warnings of the locals who treat Lake Turkana with great caution.

A small conical mountain—we call it the Black Pimple—marks the approach to North Horr. At this moment, it is my only landmark. Further on I am guided by long strings of camels, as well as circular piles of stones. These are ancient Galla tombs.

At the clinic, I find Sister Brigitte, bellicose as ever, and on the warpath.

"So you're back to fetch your patient?"

I gauge the situation. She's decided that he's my patient and nothing to do with her. So be it. I find my shepherd. Old Fellow is still wearing his terra-cotta-coloured rags, but after a night of treatment, food and sleep he looks in much better shape. He greets me serenely, as if there had been no doubt in his mind that I would return to pick him up.

Before leaving, I raid the mission shop, stocked with the local specialty—attractive basketware woven from the ubiquitous doum palm tree. I am convinced this local industry needs to be encouraged, so I try to set a good example by buying up baskets, table-mats and coasters, which fill my house, and which I give to friends and guests. I am sure that if only one of Nairobi's shop-keepers would feature these local wares he could make a fortune and also help fill the coffers of the mission. Today, however, I am vexed to see that there is practically no stock left, and that some of the most attractive models in the range are missing.

"What can one do?" laments Sister Brigitte. "It is impossible to get a regular supply of these goods. The moment the women who make them get a little cash, they stop work."

So there you go. Sister Brigitte and I are well aware that the women of North Horr are not yet ready for mass production.

I help Old Fellow aboard. This time he settles into a seat and buckles on his seat belt like a seasoned traveller. During the twenty-minute flight to Maikona he appears to be entirely absorbed by the landscape. Suddenly he grunts and taps my shoulder. He seems to be dumbfounded by something he has seen. He points to the Chalbi desert, a dried-up lake glistening with salt. It is obvious he has never imagined that such a deso-late place could exist. Compared with Chalbi, the pastures of his homeland, covered with spindly thorn bushes and rocks, must seem lush and beautiful.

Maikona is a watering-hole off the road from North Horr to Marsabit. Cattle join the procession of camels on their way to the wells. This stopping place has one great advantage over all others: my plane can be taxied from the landing strip straight into the mission courtyard. I install Old Fellow in the shade of the verandah that runs the length of the mission building. He stands there, motionless, his gaze fixed on the plane. He is frightened that I may abandon him in this desolate spot. The Maikona mission is run by the colourful Father Venturino, who breeds camels and loves to go scrambling on his powerful motorcycle. He is not here today, which is a pity as I would like to have a few stern words with him about the state his dispensary is in. No doctor and only a single nurse is in attendance, and she is a young and inexperienced Gabra girl. I have to hustle her a bit to get her to organize my consultations. The wards are untidy, the medicine cupboard is bare and there are no sterile gloves, although I am pretty sure that only recently we sent a good supply. Where on earth have they gone? The young nurse hasn't a clue and mournfully shakes her head. I've a fairly shrewd idea of what has happened to them: unless a close watch is kept on all medical supplies, and particularly on sterile gloves, considered to be the last word in sartorial elegance, they tend to find their way into the hands of the local quacks and bone-setters.

Mostly women and children are cared for at this dispensary. The former arrive suffering from a variety of gynecological disorders. One might almost see these ailments as a blessing in disguise, for they are responsible for bringing African women closer to accepting the benefits of modern medicine. Sterility among African women is a terrible stigma, tantamount, almost, to a sentence of death in these particular communities. Wives soon learned the way to the health clinics where they were given antibiotics that healed them, and their example was rapidly followed by other women. Our experience was similar with babies dying of dehydration, one of the main causes of infant mortality in Africa. Internal infections caused fatal attacks of diarrhoea. The cure is very simple—we give the mothers sachets of easily administered rehydrating powder. In this way we saved, and continue to save many infants brought to us in time. The success rates of these two life-saving treatments alone justify—if justification is needed—the existence of these bush dispensaries serving a nomadic population that has no way of getting to a town to seek vital medical assistance for themselves or their children.

The radio announces that once again a violent storm is approaching Marsabit, my next stop. I shall have to stay in Maikona longer than I had planned. I am stuck here with Old Fellow, who sits stoically in his corner. I console myself with the thought that today, at least, I shall have time for lunch.

The courtyard is paved with crushed black lava. The sun blazes down on the young acacia trees which don't as yet provide any shade. Their spindly trunks are encased in a kind of iron corset to protect them from the ravages of hungry goats. The schoolchildren, all in uniform, are playing in the courtyard. The girls wear blue skirts and pink blouses, while the boys are in blue shirts and yellow shorts. Whenever I see mission schoolchildren, I cannot help wondering what kind of future will be theirs. At present they are getting what amounts to a European education. Later on, when they are adults, they won't want to tend the family flocks and herds—indeed they may well have forgotten how to do so. They will move away from their traditional lifestyle, and drift to the towns, where they will not find work. All their book learning will only have produced an urban population of unemployed drop-outs. Would it not be more sensible to award bursaries to the brightest scholars with the best scholastic records? The less gifted children could be taught improved methods of hygiene and more sophisticated and advanced farming methods. But I suppose such an approach would smack of elitism, which is frowned upon by most governments, including those in Africa.

By two o'clock I am ready to leave, accompanied by my old shepherd who shadows my every step. The plane, which has been standing in the torrid sun for three hours, stinks like a Chinese junk, which is not surprising given that it is carrying a small cargo of dried fish from Lake Turkana, a gift from Father Mario at Loyangalani, who is aware of my passion for this particular delicacy. I had put them in the front compartment. It is high time I got going.

Half an hour later I land at Marsabit. A few steaming puddles on the runway are the only trace of the recent deluge. An ambulance is standing by and, knowing it is for him, Old Fellow turns to me for his crook and his wooden pillow, then clasps my hands in his own. As he walks to the ambulance, his sandals, made from old tire rubber, make a slapping noise on the tarmac. What, I wonder, is on his mind? Surely, he realizes that this is a big town, and that if it is possible to save his life it is here that it will be saved.

During the two-and-a-half-hour flight back to Nairobi I conjure up a mental balance sheet of my medical activities to date this year. In this district I will have seen 1,000 patients and carried out 700 vaccinations. In twenty-five years I will have accomplished 200 round trips. None have been the same, and those in the future will again be different. I shall meet other doctors and nurses. Owing to various factors, such as contracts, work permits, climate and loneliness, medical teams are never permanent. I will be faced with a variety of illnesses, and will be at the mercy of a capricious climate.

Three months later, torrential rains prevent my landing on the soaked landing strips of Dukana and Maikona. At Ileret there are sudden outbreaks of tuberculosis, acute rheumatism, malnutrition and, to cap it all, one of the nurses has been AWOL for weeks. My usual runway at North Horr has become a river, so I'll have to use another one much farther away.

I very much regret not having been able to look after Old Fellow myself. His transfer is contrary to our usual policy: it is not our role to supply hospitals in the towns with patients from distant places. On the contrary, our rule is to care for them as close to their homes as possible. We are used to making on-the-spot diagnoses and then carrying out the necessary treatment, providing, of course, we have what we need to do so.

When I first began to practise in the fifties, I had an experience that confirmed the importance of these principles. My surgery was then on my farm. I was asked to visit a sick woman who was running a high temperature. She was indeed very feverish and seemed partially paralysed. I diagnosed spinal meningitis, but as I was not entirely certain of my skill as a diagnostician, I decided to take my patient to the nearest hospital, at Nakuru, where they would be able to confirm my diagnosis. At that time the staff were all European.

"It's meningitis," I said to the young houseman on duty, "and she needs a massive dose of antibiotics."

"Really?" he answered casually. "We'll see about that."

I felt I hadn't convinced him, but I had not yet realized that townee doctors, filled with their own theories, do not take a country doctor's diagnosis very seriously. So my patient had to undergo a series of sophisticated tests, during which she died. Had I followed my own gut diagnosis and given her the antibiotics from my surgery, she might have survived. I learned a bitter lesson that day.

I must admit that I love the hours I spend in the shade of my aircraft, or under a shady tree, behind a little table covered with medicines of all kinds. The crowds surge around the table calling out the Swahili name they have given me—"Mama Daktari," Madam Doctor. Sometimes they add "N'dege," which means both bird and plane. Masses of children scamper about until they are grabbed by the nurses who must vaccinate them. The mothers present the vital vaccination certificates, which are in perfect order, if somewhat crumpled and stained. The patients peer over one another's shoulders, listening carefully to everything that is said, not wanting to miss a word. Often the noise is so loud that it is impossible to concentrate. Then I produce my Big Voice and order instantly returns.

The concept of the queue system means absolutely nothing here. Some patients try to slip past the queue a second time to get to me, either to make sure they have understood their treatment, or to get a further supply of the magic tablets I distribute in paper cones, on which the directions for use are written in symbols. Five lines and two tiny circles means two tablets a day for five days, and this system works perfectly.

The sudden flare-up of malaria in Maikona worries me. Malaria is the nightmare of tropical medicine. Westerners don't realize it is one of humanity's greatest scourges. According to the World Health Organization, at any given time a hundred million people have malaria, and two million a year die of it. Our only defence against this disease is preventive education. We try to promote the use of the humble but effective mosquito net, at least for children, who are the most at risk; the female Anopheles mosquito that transmits the disease only bites at night. It is also important to drain and infill the puddles—prime breeding grounds for mosquitoes—that are found in and around the huts in most African villages.

It is not easy to persuade people to change their habits or to adopt new ones. A team of health visitors once came to a village to explain the mechanics of infection. To back up their lecture they erected a screen on which they projected a much-enlarged picture of a mosquito. At the end of the lecture, the village chief rose to thank the health visitors.

"All this is very interesting," he said politely, "but somehow we do not feel that your lecture and photographs really concern us. You see, we don't have giant mosquitoes like that in our village."

Visitors I bring to the Northern Desert for the first time are surprised at finding missions here. They imagine them to be a hangover from the old colonial days when the work of the missionary was to convert the heathen and save their souls by bringing them into the Christian church. On the contrary, these mission stations are a fairly recent addition to the countryside. One could almost say I witnessed their birth after the Proclamation of Independence in 1963.

Under colonial rule, the British strongly discouraged the establishment of missions, believing that the indigenous population should preserve their own cultures intact, without the risk of being contaminated by European religious beliefs. The outcry raised by the white settlers when Karen Blixen took it into her head to teach Kikuyu children on her farm to read and write took a long time to die down. She was accused of trying to turn them into little English clones. A more sinister motive lay behind these accusations: according to official British thinking, educating the natives would create a threat to the lifestyle of the British settlers.

Once the British had gone, Bishop Cavalero strode onto the scene. This stocky, thickset Roman prelate, though well over sixty, was tireless in his undertakings. The Italians have always had an interest in this part of the world; at one time they had colonized Ethiopia and part of Somalia. Cavalero wanted to establish a network of Catholic missions. He badgered and bullied official bodies, district commissioners, the police and district councillors. Eventually he succeeded in persuading President Kenyatta to abolish the old restrictions imposed by the colonial regime, and he was free to evangelize to his heart's content.

Sololo is an excellent example of his particular technique. He set up a meeting with local chieftains, most of whom, ironically, were Muslim.

"You want a doctor and a hospital here? Fine. I will build you a hospital that will be staffed by nurses, and those nurses will, of course, be nuns. They will naturally want to hear Mass, and this will mean the presence of a priest. So I shall build a church, a mission station and then a hospital."

Cavalero began his building project in 1966. Wearing cement-stained dungarees, he was to be seen tirelessly superintending the building of two houses, one for the priests, the other for the nuns. The hospital was completed in 1968. It was a fine, well-constructed building, but it remained empty well into 1969—there was no sign of a doctor or of patients.

At a district meeting of the NGOs (non-governmental organizations), attended by government representatives to assess the medical development of the region, I asked Cavalero whether the hospital was in use.

Looking me full in the face, daring me to say he was lying, he said, "It is fully operational!"

"Are you sure?" I asked, but I did not press the point. I was well aware that the hospital was the least of his worries, and even today his church has not provided the funds to run the clinic. Patients pay what they can afford, the hospital is staffed by nuns sent out by their particular Order, and the doctors are provided by an Italian NGO, the C.C.M., the Comitato Collaborazione Medico, of Turin.

Not only was the hospital empty, but so was Sololo's enormous church. It was Father Davoli, a robust peasant from

Piedmont, who took on the task of filling it with worshippers. This was not easy in a place populated mainly by Muslims and animists. However, the wily father had a plan. He asked that bundles of worn clothing be sent him from Italy and he bought tools—shiny spades and hatchets—which he presented as gifts to members of the congregation as they filed out after Mass. The big church was filled to capacity, though mainly, it must be said, by shopkeepers, and the very next day Father Davoli's splendid gifts were on sale in the local shops.

It is 5 p.m. on Wednesday. I land on runway zero seven at Wilson and go straight to my office. My own mail, which I never have time to answer, is piled high in layers. There is a formidable amount of paperwork to be done in connection with my work, reports to be written, forms to be filled out and invoices to be signed. We seem to have inherited the British mania for paperwork, which I feel is sometimes carried to extremes. This is not my cup of tea, but I have two days' wait before I can go back to my refuge, my farm at Subukia.

Chapter 2

FROM ADEN TO ADDIS

Spoerry is a Swiss name that is correctly pronounced "Shpeuri," though in France only Alsatians get it right. Originally natives of Fischentahl, at the end of the Middle Ages the Spoerry clan settled at Maennedorf, a small town on the north shore of Lake Zurich. My great-grandfather, Henry Spoerry, became his community's benefactor by waging war against the worrying preponderance of alcoholics in the town. He bought up all the cafés and bars he could find and turned them into viable commercial assets—the oldest became an old-age home that is still in existence. As a reward for his public-spirited activities, he was made a freeman of the town, a privilege extended to all his descendants, which gives us, as a family, the assurance of a peaceful and friendly place in which to end our days. It is a comforting thought that there is at least one place in the world I can always find sure refuge.

Around 1848, Great-grandfather Henry, recognizing the potential of the Industrial Revolution and the development and expansion of mechanization, founded a textile firm in Alsace that soon expanded into a large, flourishing commercial enterprise. On the slope of a hill overlooking Mulhouse, in the rue du Sundgau, he built a family mansion in the English style; and it was here that I grew up, with my brother and two sisters. We took our first steps and played our first children's games in the shade of the beech and ancient cedar trees in its park.

After the annexation of Alsace in 1871, because my family was considered to be Swiss, we were allowed to keep our factory going, albeit on what had now become German soil. When the First World War broke out in 1914, my father, who had done his military service in the Swiss Army, was called up as an artillery officer. At that time everyone thought the war would soon be over, but in 1915 my father realized that it was only just getting started and decided that as an Alsatian subject he should be fighting the enemy on French soil, so he enlisted in the Foreign Legion as a Swiss national. The French, having accepted him as a Frenchman, transferred him to the 54th Artillery Regiment, in which he remained throughout the war. Although he was in the thick of some of the fiercest fighting—at Verdun and Le Chemin des Dames—and his regiment suffered enormous losses, he came through unscathed, only to nearly die in the 1919 epidemic of Spanish flu.

After the war Father returned to the responsibilities of running his factories in Mulhouse, which he had taken over at the age of twenty when my grandfather died. To take over the business he had had to interrupt his studies—he was reading maths at the University of Zurich—and then spent a year in the United States learning the cotton trade. His bent for mathematics remained with him always, and during the war he had worked out mathematical tables that made it easier to control artillery fire.

In 1914, my mother, *née* Jeanne Schlumberger, and her three-year-old son, my brother François, had taken refuge in Cavalaire in the Var region of France. So, owing to the hazards of war, I was born in the south of France, on 13 May 1918, in Cannes. Cavalaire was in the depths of the country at that time and my mother wisely decided to have me in a town where she would be safe and well looked after, so my parents leased the Villa St. Honarat on the Croisette at Cannes. Their bedroom overlooked the sea, and one of the first sights I saw from my cradle was the Mediterranean, which I have loved ever since.

My parents shared this passion and, once the war was over, they would spend Easter and the summer holidays at Cavalaire.

We used to stay at the Hotel de Pardigon, a big building at the end of a long avenue lined with palm trees. The garden was filled with olive trees that I would climb like a little monkey. I loved this place, which was owned by a Swiss family called Defago. The parents ran the hotel, and their son was the chef. All that is left of this hotel today is the great avenue of palms; the building itself was pulled down to make way for a modern block of flats.

My sister Thérèse was born in 1923, Martine in 1925. In view of these welcome additions to our family, Father began thinking about building a holiday house. He had found a suitable site close to the beach, near the hotel, in 1923, on which he wanted to build a traditional Provençal *bastide* rather than a popular-style Mediterranean villa with patios and arches. An architect in St. Raphael was chosen, and he and François, my sixteen-year-old brother, who was passionately interested in architecture, collaborated on the plans for the new house.

At this point François had not decided to make architecture his career—he wanted to join the Navy. After sitting his entry exam for the Naval School, he sailed to New York in the Merchant Navy cadet training ship *Jacques Cartier*. A slight problem with his eyesight, however, forced him to abandon the idea of a naval career, which he did without undue regret—he had quickly learned that life as a ship's officer involved more routine than adventure. He decided to become an architect and, thirty years later, was able to combine his great love of the sea and sailing with architecture by creating the marvellous lagoon village Port Grimaud, in the Bay of St. Tropez.

It may sound trite to say I admired my father, but I believe we had good reason to do so. He was tall, with a commanding presence allied to a sweet and gentle nature. He was christened Henry, like his grandfather, but everyone called him Papo. As well as being a successful industrialist, he was also a man of immense culture, particularly interested in dead languages, and a brilliant Hellenist. We were lucky to have him as our guide and mentor on our first voyage to Greece, for he inculcated in his teenage children a thirst for knowledge, for the sea and for travel.

Father was a committed Anglophile and wanted his children to speak perfect English. At Mulhouse we had an English governess to teach us the language of Shakespeare, and we were made to speak English at the table, so that by the age of five I was able speak it quite well. Father was interested in antiquities and hoped that I might one day study History of Art at Oxford. To give me a further grounding in English and also, I suspect, because I was a far from exemplary pupil at the school I was at in Mulhouse, Papo sent me to boarding school in London for two years, from 1930 to 1932.

The Francis Holland Church of England School for Girls in Graham Terrace had three hundred pupils, but there were only twenty boarders, lodged in a large house in West Eaton Place, near Sloane Square. If Father's plan of sending me to England was a form of punishment, I can only say that far from being miserable or homesick, I was blissfully happy. The English way of life suited me perfectly and I had a wonderful time.

We boarders cannot have been easy to manage, for we were a turbulent group, up to all manner of tricks. Looking back, I must admit that some of these were really rather reprehensible: for instance, one of my friends thought it a great lark to phone a funeral parlour and order a coffin to be sent to our headmistress. Since we lived in a private house, nobody questioned the arrival of the coffin, which was duly delivered to the unfortunate victim. Hidden nearby, we watched her horrified reaction with glee.

I went back to secondary school in Mulhouse in time to begin the term in Class 3. My English was good, but my Latin had been neglected—it was not, then at any rate, taught very well at Francis Holland. I had replaced Latin with German, which my parents spoke fluently, having had to learn it at the time that Germany annexed Alsace; nevertheless I really had very little interest in it. My mother belonged to the generation whose daughters were educated at home, and every year German inspectors visited private houses to make certain that their scholastic standards were being maintained and that German was spoken in the home. But after the Armistice in 1918 German was banished from our home, and very rarely did I hear my parents speaking it. However, it was in our school curriculum and there was no way I could avoid taking lessons with the rest of my class.

In Mulhouse I mixed with people who spoke Alsatian, while at Maennedorf most people spoke Swiss-German. By the time I took my "Bac," I was thoroughly confused and flunked the exam first time round, largely on account of my poor German. To put me back on track, I was sent to spend the Easter vacation at Scanfs, a Swiss village in the High Engadine. I stayed with the local pastor and his family, who spoke both Romanche (a curious language with Latin roots) and German. It was cold and there was lots of snow. I did get a little skiing in, but most of my time was spent being thoroughly crammed by the pastor's wife, so that in a comparatively short time I had mastered the basic elements of German. The presbytery was a large chalet, the first floor of which was reserved for the family while the ground floor was occupied by their cattle, which provided the heating for the entire household.

I knew that Father hoped I would opt for an academic career, but the groves of academe did not inspire me. Being brought up with my brother, sharing his games and his passion for sailing, had turned me into something of a tomboy. The country house at Pardigon had been completed in 1930 and in September we left la Bastide for the family home at Maennedorf, where my brother and I spent most of our time sailing on Lake Zurich in a fragile cockleshell of a boat called *La Coquille*. François piously preserved this tiny craft as a sort of relic, and many years later he suspended it from the roof of his boathouse at Port Grimaud.

Later on, at Cavalaire, we had the use of a more seaworthy dinghy, in which we lightheartedly skimmed the rocks, often narrowly avoiding a watery grave. No one in Cavalaire other than François and I wanted to sail; people must have thought us slightly deranged. Dragging the boat up the beach to safety every evening left us in a state of total exhaustion. The weather at Easter was not always good, and quite often there were violent storms and huge waves. One night, one of these waves carried off our dinghy, which we hadn't pulled far enough up the beach. The next morning, to our joy, we found our craft miraculously intact, firmly secured by its anchor only a few yards from the reefs.

My interest in medicine had already manifested itself in early childhood, when my first patient was my rag doll on whom I operated, opening up her stomach and then carefully sewing her up again. However, my urge to make it my career remained quiescent until the end of my year of reading Philosophy at Strasbourg, when it returned with such intensity that I made up my mind that I definitely wanted to study medicine.

I had just had a bad attack of viral hepatitis, and was still bright yellow when I went to take my "bac," which corresponded roughly to today's A-levels. A family friend, Françoise Dautheville, was an intern at Strasbourg Hospital. She looked after me and it was to her that I first confided my decision to become a doctor. At that time, few women opted for a career in medicine and I needed to talk to someone who would bolster my confidence and support my decision.

Françoise was very supportive, but I had not said anything of my plans to my parents. In September 1937, having passed my exams with flying colours, I went off to Paris to study at the Faculty of Sciences where I was to prepare for another very important examination—in Physics, Chemistry and Biology. These "premed" exams were the "open sesame" to the primary stage of studying medicine, though they could also be the lead-in to other courses—I was not yet irretrievably committed. However, when I went home for Christmas, I chatted to a neighbour, who asked me whether I had yet chosen a career. Without hesitation I answered that I was very tempted to study medicine. Having no idea that I had not told my parents of my intentions, our neighbour trotted off to discuss my future career with them. They were astonished, not that I wanted to become a doctor, but that I had kept my plans a secret, but from that time onward they were encouraging and supportive in every way.

During the Easter holidays in 1938, I went on my first big sea voyage, a two-week cruise of the Mediterranean, organized by a group of medical students. I had been invited to join them by Claude Seyrig, then an intern in a Paris hospital. The group was made up of twelve young budding medics. I had not yet reached their elevated status as I was just starting my premed studies and was very much the junior "makee learn."

We embarked in the transatlantic liner *Champlain*. The price of the cruise was reasonable, and although we travelled steerage, like emigrants to America, we were given the run of the ship, and everyone ate together. We were supposed to land in North Africa, but the weather was so bad that we sailed straight on to Beirut, and then to Syria, where Claude Seyrig had a cousin who was the director of the French Archeological School. We visited the Bekaa Valley by car, and also Damascus. After a night on the road, we reached Palmyra, and made our way to the Great Temple of the Sun just as dawn was breaking. In the middle of the night we had reached a pass that overlooked the desert and seen in the distance the camp lights of the engineers prospecting for oil. The air was so clear that the encampments seemed quite near, and we were astonished to be told that one of the camps was twenty-five, and the other sixty miles away.

Syria was then under French mandate. We were invited to a dance by spahi officers, where a White Father who did not dance wound up the gramophone for us. Then, off we went again, towards Homs, where enormous "norias," or waterwheels, lifted the waters of the Oronte to irrigate fields under cultivation. We visited the Krak des Chevaliers, the great Crusader fortress, before rejoining the ship at Aleppo. From there we sailed to Ephesus on the Turkish coast, and then on to Greece. We went ashore at Athens, Delos, Mykonos and Santorini. Finally, we sailed back to Marseilles.

It was in the Greek Islands that I noticed how clumsily the crew of the *Champlain* handled the ship. They had not been trained to work in the Mediterranean—they were used to the Atlantic—and had absolutely no idea how to launch the tenders used to ferry passengers from ship to shore. We were practically blown into the port of Marseilles—so violent was the mistral—and the enormous liner was pushed against the quay, damaging her hull.

The following year, Easter 1939, the same group of young

medical students again embarked on a cruise, this time on the *Champollion*, a liner far better equipped for cruising the Med. We planned to visit Petra during the Easter holidays the following year, but Fate was to decide otherwise.

These first voyages made a deep and lasting impression on me. I was to be forever drawn to the desert, to the civilizations of the Orient and the Middle East, but, most importantly, the travels I had undertaken helped me to overcome the later hardships of prison and the concentration camps. When I had doubts about surviving these terrible ordeals, I would seek comfort in the memory of the wonderful sights I had seen and the fact that I had not wasted my short life, but had gained both profit and pleasure from all I had seen and done.

I passed my premed exams after spending a year in a boarding house in the rue Denfert-Rochereau in Paris, an eminently forgettable place, remembered only because I was always freezing cold and the food was poor. The start of the scholastic term found François and me sharing a little flat on the Quai Voltaire, near the Beaux Arts, where he was studying architecture. The flat was conveniently close to the Faculty of Medicine where I was attending lectures. I ended my first year as a non-resident student at the Salpêtrière Hospital on a neurosurgical ward and then joined my parents at Cavalaire for the summer holidays. It was here, at the beginning of September 1939, that one of our English friends, a retired RAF officer, told us war had been declared.

My parents decided to remain at Pardigon with my two young sisters, while I returned to Paris to continue my studies. François, with four of his friends from the Beaux Arts, was sailing to Greece aboard his beloved thirty-five-foot yacht *Colibri*. This was not just a holiday, as he had managed to convince the then Minister of National Education, Jean Zay, to give him an assignment in Greece. His mission was to compile an inventory of all the principle features and characteristics of vernacular architecture in Greece.

After sailing along the Italian Coast and through the straits of Messina the young crew of architects were unable to get through the Canal of Corinth as it had been damaged by an earthquake, so they skirted the Peloponnese as far as Athens using as a chart a map from a school atlas.

Having visited the Cyclades, *Colibri* anchored off the island of Santorini, where its crew were treated to the awesome spectacle of a magnificent full-scale volcanic eruption. It was here that François and his friends heard that hostilities had begun, and that mobilization was in full swing. In order to hasten their journey back to their respective units, François entrusted *Colibri*, together with all the documentation, paperwork and reports they had assembled, to Greek friends, who undertook to sail his craft back to Athens. Unfortunately they were shipwrecked en route and *Colibri* sank. The crew were saved, but all the precious notes and papers were lost.

On arriving in France, François went straight to the barracks at Angers, where he was put in charge of recruits, to whom he taught the rudiments of saffer engineering. Then, after a few months at Versailles to obtain his commission, he was sent to the Somme where he fought until the Armistice was declared. After being demobilized, he went to Marseilles to continue his architectural studies at the Beaux Arts and to prepare for his diploma, which he obtained in 1942. The theme he chose for his examination thesis was, as might have been expected, "A Naval Dockyard."

In mid-June 1940 the Germans entered a Paris deserted by the French government, and emptied of its inhabitants, who were fleeing southwards in wave upon wave of terrified refugees. Those who lived through these dark times will remember the feelings of anger and humiliation that were aroused by the sight of Hitler's soldiers on parade in the Champs-Elysées and the Place de la Concorde. What incensed and hurt me most was the sight of the swastikas on the great banners that waved everywhere: over the Arc de Triomphe, in the rue de Rivoli and on every building the Germans had taken over for their headquarters or offices.

I continued with my studies and my work in the hospital. The Parisians gradually crept back after their useless exodus and tried to adapt to life under the Occupation, something they had never thought possible. My impression was that most people employed the only weapon left to them—indifference. They ignored the Germans, pretending they were invisible or transparent.

The Army of Occupation was, however, far from invisible, and the slightest incidents would bring jackboots running. I heard on the grapevine that a demonstration was being planned for the eleventh of November at the Arc de Triomphe. The Unknown Soldier's tomb was already heaped with a mass of flowers and the Germans guarding the tomb were obviously getting edgy. Then we heard that further reinforcements were on their way up to the Etoile. A man wearing a tricolour scarf came forward and tried to get the crowd to disperse. Realizing that we might soon be caught up in a dangerous situation, a friend and I took refuge in a nearby café on the Champs-Elysées. It was mainly patronised by gay men who, oblivious of the commotion outside, made it abundantly clear that they did not approve of girls invading their sanctuary.

Thinking back on that time in Paris, it seems to me that we were stunned, as if the skies had fallen on our heads. It was beyond belief that a nation whose subjects had for centuries fought and died in the name of *liberté*, should now be deprived of it by a foreign army. We simply could not come to terms with having our peaceful lives so violently shattered. It is also as if my memory went into hibernation, as I recall little of the major events of that period, though I can quite clearly recollect the pin-pricks and petty hassles that made our daily life so difficult.

One day, near the Luxembourg, a young woman approached me and discreetly offered to sell me some sugar. The black market was by then firmly established. I accepted the deal, and she held out a paper bag for me to taste the contents. It was real sugar. I paid, put my purchase carefully into the saddlebag on my bicycle and pedalled off to Smith's bookshop in the rue de Rivoli. Propping my bike against a wall, I went in. When I came out, I saw, with dismay, that my bike had fallen over, and my precious sugar had spilled all over the inside of the saddlebag. I then realized that the spilt powder bore little resemblance to sugar. I tasted it again: it was salt. Only the top had been sprinkled with sugar to whet the buyer's interest. It was a classic scam but a new one on me. Furious at having been duped, I rushed back across the Seine to find the black marketer. I found her looking for other mugs and, after a stormy session, she gave me back my money. In revenge I kept the salt.

Another time I was cycling home from the hospital with a bottle of pure alcohol from which I hoped to make some excellent gin for my friends. As I pedalled merrily along, I was stopped by a French policeman. Having questioned me, he searched my saddlebag and confronted me with the bottle. I knew I was in serious trouble but managed to make up what seemed to me to be a very convincing story.

"As you can see, officer, I have just come from the Salpêtrière, where I am a medical student, and I need this spirit to treat the patients I am about to visit in their homes."

The policeman did not seem too convinced by my story, but he said, "Okay, you can go. In any case we're not interested in that stuff. Tonight we're on the lookout for weapons."

My next brush with authority occurred near the Faculty of Medicine. I was on my way home to our apartment on the Quai Voltaire carrying a big parcel of books. I was stopped by a plain-clothes policeman, who asked me to open my parcel. When I did so the books slipped out of my grasp and cascaded all over the pavement. The man apologized profusely and helped me gather them up, and then offered to help me carry them home. I don't think this was just gallantry—I suspect he wanted to know where I lived, as to him anyone carrying so many books must be a suspicious character.

I was by now the only member of my family living in the Occupied Zone, and each time I wanted to visit my relatives almost insuperable difficulties had to be overcome. As a member of the Medical Faculty, I had been issued with the *Ausweis*, a pass which allowed me to circulate more freely than most people but did not allow me to cross the demarcation line between the Occupied and Non-Occupied zones. In order to get from one to the other, one was obliged to use alternative, little-known routes and to employ a guide and a variety of ruses that were not without danger. I had quite a few near misses with authority.

In the summer of 1940, well aware of the risks I was running, I managed to get a train to the south, where I joined my parents and my two sisters, who had taken refuge at Cavalaire. Planning my return to Paris was a major operation. From Toulon I took the train to Brive, where I was to await the arrival of Claude Seyrig and her husband. They were going to drive me back to Paris. I was to provide the petrol, fuel being number one on the list of rationed commodities. Furthermore, petrol was as rare as gold dust, even in what was laughingly known as the Free, or Unoccupied, zone—to us, the "Zone Nono."

Having secured two five-litre cans of petrol, I stowed them carefully in my backpack. I arrived at the station early enough to find two empty compartments, placed my backpack in the rack of one and found a seat next door in the other. I had carefully planned this manoeuvre: carrying fuel was forbidden, but I reckoned that if I sat elsewhere nobody would connect me with my backpack. From time to time during the journey, I kept a discreet watch on my cargo by sauntering up and down the corridor. Apart from a strong smell of petrol spreading through the carriage, caused no doubt by the heat in the train, nobody seemed to have noticed my backpack or its contents.

On arriving at Brive, I was in for another traumatic experience. I had expected to be met by my friends, but there was no sign of them. Uneasy and bewildered, I went and sat on the steps outside the station. Claude was always punctual. What could have happened to her and to her husband, and what was I going to do in this unknown town with my dangerous load of fuel? To my immense relief, eventually I spotted my friends' little SIMCA 5 coming down the street.

They had lost their way. The car was a small two-seater and I had to fit in as best I could. I managed to wedge my then skinny frame into the back of the car in between the petrol cans. Claude and her husband had prepared a detailed route map so as to avoid roadblocks, and in due course and without any mishaps we reached the Loire, the frontier of the Occupied Zone. There the Germans examined our papers. There was no problem. Our *Ausweissen* were in order, so without further delay we were allowed to cross the frontier. Since we were low on petrol, we asked whether it was possible to top up.

"The pump is over there," said one of the soldiers, adding courteously, "you can buy as much fuel as you want."

The war had only just begun, and as yet the occupying forces lacked for nothing, but as the enemy tightened its grip things went from bad to worse. The struggle for survival was on, and silent resistance was the order of the day. François had made contact with Dr. Jean Bernard, head of various Resistance networks in the south of France. He was later to become a famous professor and member of the Academy. Bernard's network was in touch with those of Colonel Maurice Buckmaster, head of the French Section of the Special Operations Executive (SOE). From London, Buckmaster organized all the secret sabotage operations and parachute landings in France; his office co-ordinated the intelligence collected in France by his agents. It was Churchill himself who, as early as July 1940, had laid the groundwork and rules for S.O.E., which operated independently of the Army and of British Intelligence. In London, Buckmaster recruited the men and women who volunteered to work for the SOE. Those who were chosen were parachuted into Occupied France. They needed special qualities, among which were courage, determination and a cool head. Most importantly, they had to be fluent in French. A third of the recruits were French or Anglo-French; the others were British, Canadian, American, or Mauritian.

Between 1941 and 1944, Buck's organization parachuted 366 officers into enemy territory. Approximately 4,000 people worked for the SOE and for us in France. Our particular job was to locate suitable sites for the parachute landings, and to find safe houses for new arrivals. We also had to establish and investigate makeshift runways to allow the Lysanders to land unobserved. These small planes, built of light wood, were popularly supposed to be able to land on a sixpence. They could carry the pilot and two passengers. The secret landings by Lysander made it possible to equip the Maquis with weapons and explosives, and to evacuate agents who had accomplished their missions. Hitler was aware of the damage this inflicted on his occupying forces. It was said that in the event of a German invasion of England, number three on their blacklist would have been Buckmaster. Fate had other ideas, however, for the colonel lived until April 1992, when he died peacefully at the age of ninety.

In the meantime, François had set up office in the Hotel d'Espagnet, one of the big houses on the Cours Mirabeau in Aix-en-Provence. The office was a blind, as the house was in fact being used as a hideout, and weapons belonging to members of François's network were stashed away amidst fake rafters. Officially, my brother was doing research on the traditional architecture of Provence, which gave him an excellent excuse for moving around freely without arousing suspicion.

My role in Paris was to run a safe house, and to look after the SOE people coming from London. I acted as a kind of liaison officer, and it was up to me to make the necessary arrangements to get the new arrivals to their various destinations. Jean Bernard, in his book *C'est de l'homme qu'il s'agit (This Concerns Man)*, has fully described what those years of passion and anguish meant, as well as our crazy adventures, and the mounting anguish and fear of the net closing in on us.

As in all the Resistance networks there were rash ventures, and treachery. On 17 April 1943, François was arrested at Aix. He was held for several months in Fresnes prison and then sent on a round of concentration camps, beginning with Naue-Bremme, the Struthof then on to Buchenwald and Dora. Finally, he ended up in Dachau, and it was there he heard the news of the landings in Normandy and Provence. He was freed in May 1945 when Allied troops liberated the camp.

I was arrested a few days after François while I was at work in the Hérold Hospital. I was incarcerated in Ravensbrück, from which I was freed on the twenty-fifth of April, when the camp was emptied by the Swedish Red Cross, thanks to the intervention of Count Bernadotte. Five days later Hitler committed suicide. The horrors of Ravensbrück are described in detail in Germaine Tillion's book *Ravensbrück*. It is, I believe, the definitive work on the subject.

In August 1944 my parents, already in the depths of despair, were subjected to a further cruel blow. The Germans, anticipating the possibility of an Allied landing in Provence, decided to destroy any building that might be of use to an invader and la Bastide de Pardigon, our seaside house, just fifty yards from the beach, was immediately targeted for demolition. My family had been forewarned of this and been given permission to remove anything portable. So they stripped the place clean of furniture, doors, windows, fittings and even bathroom fixtures and put everything into the safe keeping of our cousins in Cavalaire.

The Germans then methodically razed the house to the ground, though as it was solidly built it took them some time do so. Ironically, thorough as ever, they cleared a wide path which allowed the Americans who landed on the coast on the fifteenth of August to drive their armoured cars straight up from the beach through the ruins of Pardigon.

Later, my father collected all the signs, placards and notices scattered far and wide by the advancing Allied troops. When the house was eventually rebuilt, all these souvenirs were housed together under the vast porch in the courtyard. There they remain to this day, a humble but moving memorial to the landings in Provence.

The rebuilding of Pardigon was, for us all, symbolic of a new beginning, a life that had been given back to us like a wonderful and unexpected gift. François concentrated all his energy and talent on his work as an architect until, firmly closing the door on the past, he decided to marry and found a family. The bride he chose was Joy, one of the daughters of our friend and neighbour Antonin Besse at Cavalaire.

Those familiar with the works of the writer Henri de Monfried may remember that in his second book, *Aventures de mer*, the author tells of meeting with Besse, then already the head of the most important commercial enterprise in Aden, in 1917. Born in Carcassonne in 1899, at twenty-two Besse became a clerk in the trading company that, twenty years earlier had employed another young clerk, Arthur Rimbaud, one of France's most illustrious poets. It did not take Besse long to start up his own business, hazardous as such an undertaking was for those who were not loyal subjects of His Britannic Majesty in a British colony. He was, however, an exceptional individual and he soon laid the foundations of his great fortune by trading in, and controlling the sale of, all colonial produce, bartered or sold, between the African ports and those of the Middle East. Besse bought, sold or transported animal skins, spices, essential oils, salt, cigarettes, cotton, ivory and petrol, as well as a great many other articles and commodities that I have forgotten.

Every summer Antonin Besse, nicknamed "Anto" or just A.B., left the oppressive heat of Aden to rejoin his family in Europe. In 1925 he had fallen in love with Le Paradou, a farm high in the hills above Pardigon. At first he rented the property; later, when the owners were willing to sell, he bought it and Le Paradou became his second home. Besse was deeply attached to his farm, and often said that if paradise really existed, God must have modelled it on Le Paradou.

As our holidays and those of the Besse children were spent at Cavalaire, we grew up together, and, oddly, it was the marriage of my brother to a childhood friend and daughter of a family with whom we had always been close that was to set my feet on the path to far countries. De Monfried's books had already fired my imagination, and combined with the stories Anto told me of his travels between Ethiopia, Arabia and the Yemen, they sowed seeds in my mind that grew and blossomed. I was certain that one day I would live in such a country, and this knowledge had been strengthened by the trials and hardships of the war. I dreamed particularly of settling in Ethiopia, for de Montfried's description of this strange, distant land attracted me deeply. I longed to explore it for myself.

As soon as I had recovered my health, and healed some of the spiritual wounds left by my recent experiences, I took my finals in Paris, and then spent a year in Basle to obtain the Diploma in Tropical Medicine. The thought of getting away spurred me on. It was a time when the young longed to escape from bloody conflicts to a more peaceful world. We desperately wanted to quit shattered, broken-down old Europe and find a new life in a new continent filled with the promise of a full and tranquil existence.

In the autumn 1948 my studies were over and I was at last free to take charge of my life and to accept Antonin Besse's tempting invitation to accompany him to Aden, close to the Ethiopia of my dreams. Besse was then also the owner of a small shipping company with a fleet of about a dozen dhows and two cargo ships, the *El Hak* and the *El Amin*. All his ships sailed under his red-and-green house flag, with the initials AB in a white circle. All Anto's possessions bore his monogram, even the soap.

In October 1948 I embarked at Marseilles with Anto and Hilda, his wife, in the *El Hak*. We made a detour, via Beirut, to the Bekaa Valley, then sailed through the Suez Canal to the Red Sea. I was not disappointed: everything I saw tallied exactly with de Montfried's descriptions. I spent most of my time on the bridge with Captain Walsh, an entertaining Englishman. The chief engineer was Scottish, with an accent thick enough to cut with the proverbial knife. When we first met I could not understand a word he said—I was convinced he was speaking Danish, or some other Scandinavian tongue, until eventually the penny dropped and I realized he was speaking his mother tongue.

The 1,500-tonne *El Hak* was not exactly a luxury liner. The cabins were spartan, which did not worry me in the least as I was enchanted by my first voyage of discovery. In fact, I found the fifteen days it took to reach Aden far too short, even though we had some uncomfortable moments in the Red Sea. Our small vessel was badly shaken when we passed the *Pasteur*, a troopship carrying soldiers back to France from Indo-China. Unlike the *El Hak*, the big ship did not even notice the swell. The hold was wide open, and dozens of soldiers lay on the deck enjoying the sunshine.

Our next port of call was Jeddah in Saudi Arabia, where a hundred or so pilgrims bound for Mecca came aboard to sail with us to Aden. Since no more than ten passengers were allowed to embark unless there was a doctor on board, I became the official doctor of the *El Hak*. Each pilgrim paid twenty gold sovereigns for his passage, so transporting pilgrims was a lucrative money-spinner. Like tourists in August, the pilgrims on their journey to Mecca were exploited and squeezed like lemons. This was how, before becoming a flying doctor, I became a ship's doctor.

A few weeks later I repeated the trip, only this time I rejoined the *El Hak* at Jeddah. I flew from Aden, stopping off at Djibouti, Addis Ababa, Asmara and Port Sudan, where I had my first taste of Sudanese official red tape, though later I would have many such encounters. To enter Sudan you had to have been vaccinated against yellow fever. As the trip was a spur-of-the-moment decision, I had had my injection just before I left, and a first injection was only valid ten days later. My certificate was therefore not in order, and the Port Health Medical Officer, a man of unshakable principles, refused to antedate it. When I touched down at Port Sudan, having flown from Aden in an Aden Airways plane, nobody stopped me, and I spent the night in an hotel. The next morning, however, before leaving for Jeddah, the airport health inspector proved uncooperative.

"Your certificate is worthless. You have not complied with the strict rules governing a first injection for yellow fever, so I cannot allow you to leave."

I tried claiming that I had had a previous injection, but my tormentor was inflexible. He held up the plane's take-off and sent for his chief, an English doctor, who was furious at having been dragged from his bed at dawn.

"What's going on here? "he raged. "You should have seen that the certificate was invalid yesterday. Now that the lady has spent a night on our territory it is too late to remedy the situation. Just let her leave, now, immediately."

At Jeddah, while waiting for the *El Hak*, I spent three days with Monsieur Delaby, director of the Bank of Indo-China. He and Besse seemed to have a close working relationship—just how close I understood when I came to embark. We were about to cast off moorings when some members of Delaby's staff arrived with a small crate that was so heavy it needed two men to carry it. I learned that it was filled with gold sovereigns. At that time, all financial transactions with the Saudis were conducted in gold. Before the days of petrodollars and telexes, their transactions were on a strictly cash basis. Bankers were crushed under piles of precious metal that had to be recirculated. Through Besse, Delaby sent his gold to India, where it fetched far higher prices. I'm not entirely sure that all this juggling was legal; probably the crew were standing by to fling the crate into the sea, should any curious customs official come sniffing round. Let us be charitable and say that smuggling gold was a colourful local custom. Not so very long ago, gold for India was the main cargo of the swift and powerful dhows based in the Arab Emirates, mainly in Dubai.

Again, it was far from a luxury cruise. The pilgrims were parked on the quarterdeck, stretched out near the bridge amid their innumerable bundles. The heads, or latrines, were on the foredeck, and consisted of a platform with a hole in the middle, over the sea. When the swell was heavy, a specific time was fixed for the vessel to heave to, stern to the wind, to prevent passengers tumbling into the water while obeying the call of nature.

My main worry was the possibility of an outbreak of cholera on board. The pilgrims, in the main, were exhausted, badly nourished and had come from many far and scattered places. It did not take me long, however, to realize that from a sanitary point of view pilgrim health was strictly controlled, and that the catastrophes one might have feared among such mixed groups bound for Mecca never happened. When the ship arrived at Jeddah, an army of doctors and nurses came on board, subjecting each and every pilgrim to the most rigorous examination and making certain that all vaccination certificates were in order. The Saudis were, and still are, haunted by the fear of infectious diseases being spread by the pilgrims, which accounts for their vigilance.

Aboard *El Hak* I held two surgeries, morning and evening. My only troublesome patients were Somalis, who had an unfortunate habit of fighting one another—a habit, I may say, that persists to this day. Their creed can be summed up as follows: my clan against my tribe, my brother against my cousin; I against my brother. My medical work was limited to bandaging wounds and sewing up scalps torn during scraps between brothers and cousins.

Having called in at Moka, we caught up with the *Daoud*, one of Besse's big sailing dhows. She was having a hard time trying to beat to windward and Besse gave orders by radio from Addem for her to be taken in tow until we had passed through the Straits of Bab-el-Mandeb, after which the wind would be more favourable.

Besse made a special point of always being on the best of terms with his "nacoudas," who were not only the captains of his dhows but also experienced commercial agents, owing to their inside knowledge of local markets. They knew exactly what merchandise was needed, where it was to be found, even in the remotest ports, and what it would cost. This information was swiftly passed on to Besse, who knew exactly what to do with it. It was thanks to his knowledge of what was going on in the marketplace that he was able to build up his great fortune.

After a brief stop in Aden, we reboarded the *El Hak* again to sail to Mukallah, where we had to land a further cargo of pilgrims. Mukallah is some 125 miles further east, on the south coast of the Yemen. It was from this magnificent town that in 1934 the traveller Freya Stark, a friend of Besse, disappeared into the Hadramout to follow the Incense Trail. Red, ochre and black cliffs towered over the ancient biblical city and a multitude of dhows rocked gently on the silken waters of its harbour. I have always thought this one of the most beautiful places in the world, and whenever possible I went back there.

After the second voyage, I decided that, although I had had some interesting, not to say exciting, experiences on board, I did not want to look after the next batch of pilgrims going to or coming from Mecca. Besse gave my post to an Indian doctor who was certainly better qualified than an inexperienced young European woman for this particular work. My most prized trophy from this adventure is a certificate from the British Merchant Navy.

Around Christmas 1948, I at last discovered Ethiopia, which I had for so long dreamed of and thought of as my promised land. Hilda, Anto, and I sailed in the *Daoud* across the Gulf of Aden to Djibouti. From there I took a plane to Addis Ababa. Anto had arranged for me to accompany Mr. Davis, director of Besse enterprises in Ethiopia, on one of his tours of the country. We travelled in a jeep with a wooden box-body to visit the local agents and bring them their cash. I was sitting in the front, next to the driver. Under my feet was a large well-filled sack.

"I hope the sack is not in your way?" asked Mr. Davis politely.

"Not at all, but what's in it?"

"Maria Theresa thalers."

For centuries the Maria Theresa thaler, from which the dollar takes its name, was the official currency of the Austrian Empire whose mines in Bohemia provided them with an abundance of currency. Through the meanderings of history, the thaler became the traditional currency of the countries bordering the Red Sea. The image of the plump Empress of Austria, Maria Theresa (mother of the unfortunate last Queen of France, Marie Antoinette), was popularly supposed to be a symbol of fertility.

My feet, therefore, were resting on a fortune. The driver, whose name, like that of the Emperor, was Haile, seemed relaxed and cheerful, though I noticed he kept a revolver in the glove compartment.

"I keep it handy in case we come across the *shiftas*, he said with a big smile. "They are everywhere."

One night in the south we got lost. We had travelled all day and were tired and covered with dust. We had driven through the river Awash, cutting through herds of beasts, and herders dressed in jodhpurs and white *chamahs* holding shepherds' crooks. It was a truly biblical scene. Before nightfall, we had glimpsed the great lake of Awasa; then in the gathering darkness we took a wrong turn leading to the mountains. Edging the floodlit road were attractive bamboo fences. Eventually we came upon a police patrol.

"Are we anywhere near Dila?"

"No, you are miles away. You are going in the wrong direction. You will have to turn back. This road is closed on account of the gold mines, and this is a forbidden area."

There was nothing for it but to turn round. We finally reached Dila at dawn, where we were warmly welcomed by a representative of Anto's company, a Belgian who had once been a tram driver. He and his wife had used their slender means to make his little home, which doubled as an office, as comfortable and cosy as possible. We were so exhausted and dusty that it seemed the height of luxury to be offered a hot bath, though it was the first time I had ever taken a bath in brick-red water.

Besse's agent's work consisted mainly of buying skins and coffee. Dila was an important coffee-growing centre. Davis topped up the Belgian's cash box—a petrol drum embedded in cement with a stoutly padlocked iron door in one side—with the requisite number of thalers. There were also a few rifles around. A well had been sunk in the courtyard. Half an inner tube served as a novel kind of bucket.

The following day, travelling homewards, we drove through groves of the coffee tree plantations that grew wild in the forest. It was harvest time. In Kenya the beans are peeled, but here, owing to lack of funds, they are left to dry on the ground and our wheels simply crunched over them. On a recent visit to Uganda I saw this same somewhat unorthodox method being used.

On another occasion, while still in the south, we visited Djimma, a remote town built by the Italians. The main street looked like a film set. It was lined with magnificent buildings: bank, law court, police station and a few shops. But all these imposing facades were built of stucco, and the buildings behind them were just sheds. In Besse's agent's fine house we found pretty pink baths and toilets that had never been plumbed in.

We travelled through districts whose populations, mobilized by the Emperor, were building roads. We saw big crowds frenetically digging at the ground with hoes attached to long poles. The scene reminded us that this country was still organized along feudal lines. In three weeks my memory had accumulated a store of dramatic images far exceeding those I had dreamed about for so long. I had crossed the Danakil Plain, travelled in the lee of the Ethiopian mountain ranges and seen the suspension bridge being built over the Blue Nile. I had visited Debra—Marcos, Abba Libanos and Lalibela, where the churches were built into the living rock or perched on top of mountains, all of them decorated with strange, naive frescoes.

This was a backward country, trapped in its past like a fly in amber. Settled by early Christians and surrounded by hostile Muslims, it was immured in a natural fortress, a kind of African Tibet. "Forgetful of a world which had forgotten them," said the historian Edward Gibbon.

Ethiopia follows the Julian calendar, which means that Christmas falls in early January, and Epiphany, Christ's baptismal day, takes place twelve days later. It is at this time that the Feasts of Timkat take place. I was present on that occasion at Addis Ababa. I saw the Emperor, surrounded by high dignitaries of the church under multi-coloured canopies, watching a crowd clad in ravishing costumes dancing in an immense square.

I took the *Littorino*, a twin-engined railcar that made it possible to travel in a day from Addis to Dire Dawa. From there I drove by car to Harar, the town so dear to my hero de Montfried, and there I visited a hospital run by a French doctor. His autoclave was giving trouble, and I was able to help him repair it. I also met another doctor, Père Bernard, a missionary who spent the afternoons working in his dispensary. His fee for seeing a patient was two dollars, which was expensive. The good father stockpiled his fees in what he called his Dollar Box. He used this money to treat patients who could not afford to pay, and he bought chaulmoogra oil, a vegetable substance from India that was used at that time in the treatment of leprosy—today we use more modern drugs, such as dapsone, a chemotherapeutic agent also used in the prophylaxis of malaria. If treated in time, leprosy is no longer the scourge it was in the Middle Ages. The only problem in getting access to the patients in time to detect the signs of leprosy, and to treat it in its early stages.

The *Littorino* travelled every Sunday the route of the famous Franco-Ethiopian Railway, which links Addis to Djibouti and which, at that time, was owned by a French company. Its managing director, one Michel Cot, infuriated Besse by charging exorbitant prices for the carrying of goods. In order to outmanoeuvre him, Anto mounted one of his brilliant schemes.

For military reasons, the Italians had constructed a road from Addis to Port Assab on the borders of Djibouti, and Anto decided to make use of this. He bought a hundred tanker lorries equipped with trailers and, with the co-operation of the Shell company's Aden branch, had them loaded with fuel at Assab and then driven to Addis. Once emptied, their tanks were carefully hosed out and then loaded with a cargo of coffee. On the roofracks they carried a supercargo: lambskins from Bati on the way down and salt from the sea on the way back.

This sort of terrestrial equivalent of an airlift was highly successful as the rail tariffs were far higher than Besse's prices. At the height of his success the government of the Negus introduced their new official currency, the Ethiopian dollar, and put up the country's stock of silver thalers for sale on the world market. Besse got the contract to carry this valuable assignment, the convoy being escorted by an imposing detachment of soldiers of the Ethiopian army.

I spent a night at Dessie, in the company of the Italian lorry drivers. They had assembled near a wood of eucalyptus trees. At an altitude of 5,000 feet it was pretty chilly. The drivers collected enough wood to make a roaring fire both to keep themselves warm and to cook their supper, after which, by the light of the moon, they raised their voices and sang heartily until they were tired and trailed off to their bunks.

The big Lancia lorries travelled only by day, as the drivers were afraid of breaking down or being attacked by roving bandits; all the drivers and mechanics were armed. The journey to and from the coast took six days and the state of the roads was so appallingly bad that all the tires had to be replaced each trip.

Filled with hope of remaining permanently in this enchanting country, I applied to the government for a post as medical officer. My hopes were quickly dashed. An official letter informed me that all medical posts were filled and that there were no vacancies in the foreseeable future. To say that I was disappointed was an understatement. I was, of course, at liberty to start a private practice. I discovered that there were only twenty-nine government doctors in the whole country—a country twice the size of France with a population of 15 million souls! But where, I wondered, would I find patients in such an underdeveloped country? I could have tried my luck in the capital but I knew that I should never be happy working in a city.

On returning to Aden, I tried to forget my disappointment in a spate of hard work. The Director of Medical Services of the Colony had asked me to take over the duties of a doctor in the women's wards of the civilian hospital, which took in Arab and Indian female patients. Only a woman doctor was allowed to examine or look after Muslim women. The doctor who had previously been in charge had fallen ill and been repatriated to England. I decided to try this new adventure on a six-month contract.

The Europeans in the colony preferred to be treated in the RAF Military Hospital, whose young and pretty nurses were known, as were their counterparts in India, as the "Fishing Fleet." Many of these attractive young women completed successful "fishing" expeditions by landing husbands.

My work in the local, or "native," hospital was extremely instructive, and I met a number of unusual people there. One of these was an American woman who was one of the wives of a Yemeni sailor. She lived the traditional reclusive life of a Yemeni wife and I asked her whether she missed the freedom of life in her homeland.

"Not in the least," she replied. "Here I have everything I could possibly want or need, and I am surrounded by doting aunts and grandmothers who seem to delight in spoiling me. If you only knew what kind of life I led in the States." Although she did not enlarge on her former life, I guessed she had been "on the game" and was more than grateful to have found peace and security well away from home.

Another time my consulting room was invaded by a group of heavily veiled Arab women. I said I only saw one patient at a time, but a member of staff explained that one of the ladies in the group was the Sultana of Mukallah, and under no circumstances whatsoever were the five slaves of her entourage allowed to leave her. I was amazed that such feudal practices still existed in southern Arabia in 1949.

Tuberculosis was rife among the Arabs and, since antibiotics were still in the experimental stage, their chances of recovery from the disease were minimal, but the Director of Medical Services had devised an original and successful treatment for TB patients. They were put to bed in a vast airy ward, protected from the sun only by blinds. It hardly ever rains in Aden and they had to stay in bed, day and night, for six months. Most European patients would not have put up with such a lengthy treatment, but the Arabs seemed to enjoy the enforced bed rest, laughing and chatting amongst themselves to while away the time. They were given a very rich diet, high in calories, to which was added shark liver oil, which is a thousand times stronger than cod liver oil and is packed with vitamins. It has a revolting taste, but the accommodating patients seemed to like it and to thrive on it.

I began work at the hospital at 7 a.m. As I had no ward duties I was free to spend the afternoons as I liked. I often accompanied Anto Besse on his excursions into the countryside. We generally drove in a big Chrysler to Sheik 'Uthman, where we mounted horses awaiting us and rode off into the desert. Sometimes we went on climbing expeditions in the mountains. Anto was an experienced mountaineer and knew every crevice of the rock faces we scaled. Having reached a mountain crest, we generally came down on the other side facing the sea and in the full glory of the setting sun.

Anto was a physical fitness fanatic. All his offices closed at 4 p.m. sharp so his staff could go riding, play tennis or go swimming. He was a great admirer of the British educational system with its emphasis on sporting activities. He did not altogether agree with French educational methods, which he found too theoretical and based on the accumulation of knowledge rather than on practical matters, debate and individual assessment of a person or situation.

In his business life, Anto preferred employing young Arabs, but they were not as good at their work as their European counterparts, having had no education beyond the Koran. Anto was one of the first to realize what is well known to the entire world today: if you want to raise the level of education given to boys, you must first educate the women who look after them in the most crucial years of their childhood. Suiting the action to the word, he created and funded the first schools for Muslim girls in Aden, and kept them going in spite of hostile reactions from Arab traditionalists outraged by this departure from the old ways.

In August 1949 my contract with the hospital ended, and I had the opportunity of visiting Kenya to stay with Mary and Heron Bruce, a couple I had met in Aden who owned a small farm at Thomson's Falls in the Rift Valley where they spent their holidays. Mary was an artist, and Heron was assistant commissioner of the Aden Police. They were seasoned travellers, having met in Palestine and served also in Antigua and Guyana. Besse and Heron were great friends, and I imagine Heron was able to pass on useful intelligence amid the turbulence of the region. Anto Besse had established a well-organized network of communications that helped him enormously to make the right business decisions.

Heron had recently been involved in a worrying affair, trying to sort out a delicate situation fraught with potentially serious economic and political implications for the Yemen. As a result of the war in Palestine and the confrontation between Jews and Arabs, attacks had broken out against the Jews in the Jewish community of the Yemen. This was the last straw as far as the Jews were concerned, and they decided to emigrate to the newly created State of Israel, but the Imam of the Yemen did not want them to leave because they were an important pillar of the country's economy. They were also famous silversmiths. The Jews were adamant, however, and took refuge in Aden, where their co-religionists organized an airlift to take them to safety. It was a foreshadowing of the bold operation that saw the Falashas of Ethiopia airlifted to safety forty years later.

While all this commotion was taking place, we were returning from a ride on the heights of Sheik 'Uthman. We stopped off at Aden's Polo Club to have a drink. To get back to the town, one was obliged to take a road through the airport. When a plane was on the runway, a barrier similar to those on a level-crossing came down and warning bells rang loudly. On this particular occasion, the barriers remained firmly closed while charter planes of Alaska Airways took off almost non-stop, carrying away the Jews of the Yemen. For security reasons, the planes only took off at nightfall, which meant we were marooned in the club, which did a roaring trade.

Being pressed for time, I flew straight on to Nairobi, although I should have preferred to travel on the Uganda-Kenya railway, which ran from Mombasa, crossing the wild Tsavo plains before tackling the steep climb towards the Central Highlands. Travelling in this legendary train was the royal route to Kenya, and a journey that I was to take many times in the future. From Nairobi I drove to Thomson's Falls, where, unless one was blind or incredibly blasé, one could not fail to be impressed by the splendour of the scenery—the majestic escarpments of the Rift Valley, the splendour of the great lakes, the incredible variety of fauna in the mild climate of the Highlands. This country was as impressive as Ethiopia but infinitely richer and better developed. After fifteen days in Kenya my dream had changed course, and I knew for certain that it was here, in this lovely country, that I wanted to spend my life. Secure in this inner conviction, I returned to France and spent a further year at the Faculty of Medicine to prepare my thesis on amoebiasis, an endemic disease of tropical climes.

It was as a fully fledged doctor, then, that at the end of September 1950 I sailed for Aden aboard the *El Hak*. On arrival, the Port Captain offered to take me on to look after his staff, but it was not a very tempting offer, with poor pay and no perks, such as lodging, car or servants. I knew it was impossible to live there with only one servant, who would refuse to take on duties of a maid-of-all-work. Social pressures made it obligatory to employ a staff of at least four; a cook, gardener, night-watchman and someone to wait at the table. Since my dream of living in Ethiopia had crumbled, I might have accepted the Port Captain's offer with financial assistance from my family, but I had discovered Kenya, and had no intention of going back on my decision to settle there.

Anto Besse was far from pleased by my future plans. He felt that by leaving Aden I was letting him down. I was deeply unhappy at the thought of living far from this man who had the rare talent of giving a sparkling new dimension to life that he communicated to all around him—banishing gloom and all that was banal, but I consoled myself with the thought that Kenya was not far from Aden and that we could often meet. I had no idea that Anto had less than a year to live.

Besse had not had the advantage of a formal or classical education, something he deeply regretted, and he had made up for this by immensely wide reading. His mastery of the English language was such that his translation of Kipling's famous "If," was thought to be even better than that of André Maurois. He was a passionate lover of fine art, and had amassed a superb collection of antiquities of southern Arabia, which he bequeathed to the British Museum. During his last years, he concentrated the greater part of his energies on endowing schools and universities. Among these were technical colleges at Aden and Djibouti and the University of Addis Ababa. He carried out all his good works strictly anonymously, seeking no publicity or honours for himself—his ruling passion was education.

At the time of my first visit to Aden, Anto had just attained the goal he had set himself: to create a school based on his ideas on the education of the young. He had given up trying to establish such a school in France, where the authorities vigorously opposed his ideas, and categorically refused to contenance any changes in their educational methods. There were many other stumbling blocks in France, such as tax demands and the problems involved in the system of issuing diplomas. Worn out by his struggle, Anto had turned to England, where he founded a new college at Oxford. He did not ask that it be known as the Besse College but was happy for its name to discreetly mirror his own first name. Thus did St. Anthony's College, Oxford come into being.

In June 1951 Anto went to England to receive the Diploma of Doctor of Civil Law. He was already a Knight of the British Empire, the second highest honour the Queen can bestow on a foreign national, for Anto had always kept his French nationality. He had planned to go to Scotland after the ceremony at Oxford, to visit Gordonstoun, another of the schools he funded. On arrival, he suffered a massive stroke, and he died on 2 July 1951 at the naval base at Kinloss, near Aberdeen. He was seventy-four years old. A Guard of Honour saluted his coffin, which was then flown back to France, where his body rests in the grounds of his beloved Paradou, in the midst of the hills of Cavalaire in which he had found his earthly Paradise.

The following year Joy, François's wife, died, plunging the Besse family again into grief and mourning. She left two sons, Yves and Bernard. Peter and Tony, two of Anto's sons, continued to manage the Besse company and interests in Aden until 1967, when the British abruptly left Aden, causing panic among the inhabitants. Over a hundred thousand people—half the population—subsequently fled. As soon as Independence was declared, Besse's company was liquidated, its vast assets appropriated, and the directors, top management and staff hounded out of Aden. At least Anto was spared the pain of seeing the total destruction of his life's work.

Chapter 3

TWO FARMS IN AFRICA

When I went back to Kenya at the end of 1950, my first priority was to pull as many strings as possible to find employment as a doctor. In Nairobi the Director of Medical Services at the Ministry of Health offered me three appointments. One was in the big African maternity hospital in Nairobi, but I still did not want to live in the city, and I had no postgraduate training in obstetrics. The second post was on the coast, at Malindi, which at that time was not the tourist centre it is today, though even then many Europeans used to holiday there. However, I did not want to work in a holiday town with a rather trying climate.

The third appointment was far more interesting. It was in the north, in Marsabit District. As nomadic desert tribes and "darkest Africa" were still a part of my dreams, I immediately put in an application, causing the district commissioner at Marsabit to have a fit.

"What!" he said. "A woman doctor, and unmarried? Unthinkable. She would be a most unsettling influence on all my young officers!"

I knew that there was no way he would change his mind, so I looked elsewhere. I also knew that the farmers around Naivasha had formed a co-operative in order to be able to afford the services of a full-time doctor, to whom they would guarantee a minimum annual salary. Dr. Bunny, their present doctor, wanted to leave. The only obstacle was that the farmers were also against a

woman doctor, for which attitude they found a number of ridicu-
lous excuses. A woman, they said, would never want to go out
on night calls, would most certainly be scared of wild animals,
and heaven knew what else. In any case, Dr. Bunny decided to
stay on. I was becoming somewhat anxious about my future,
when I met up again with friends I had known in Aden who had
retired to Thomson's Falls, and they told me that the farmers of
Ol Kalou were also on the lookout for a doctor. This time no
chauvinist hurdles blocked my way. I got the job, and was to
keep it for fourteen years.

Ol Kalou lies in the green and beautiful plain that stretches
from the Aberdares to the Rift Valley. Situated at an altitude of
over 8,000 feet, it enjoys a mild and temperate climate, a kind of
eternal but misleading spring, though at that altitude one can
easily get out of breath and one tires at the least effort. But I was
only thirty-two, and quickly adapted to the height.

I leased a tiny surgery in the village and rented a house on a
farm a couple of miles away. Mary Patten, its owner, could not
do enough to make the new doctor as comfortable as possible—
it was pleasant to feel wanted.

On the very first day that I moved into my new house, I lit a
big fire in the grate, and, at about 10 p.m., having dowsed the
embers, I trotted off happily to bed. Towards two or three in the
morning, I was woken by a series of explosions and through the
crack under my bedroom door I could see a fiery red glow. I ran
out of the back door shouting "Fire!" The farm workers, carrying buckets of water, appeared almost instantly. On opening the
door of the living room we saw that a cushion of one of the arm-
chairs was burning merrily. The fire had been caused by a chunk
of damp cement from the chimney falling on the dying embers
and sending out a spark hot enough to set the cushion alight. We
took the armchair out onto the lawn, and having poured buckets of water over it, confidently believed we had put out the fire
for good. An hour later, however, it started up again. The cush-
ions were stuffed with kapok, from a local tree whose flowers are
like cotton wool. Kapok is a deadly fire hazard, for once it is

alight it is almost impossible to put out. Fortunately, at that time I had little furniture and no curtains.

I was now a country doctor covering sixty farms spread over a radius of thirty miles, so I was not short of patients. Each farmer housed his family, staff and African labour force, making a total of 100 or 200 souls per farm. The farmers took almost paternal care of the health of their employees, paying all their medical expenses. I was out at all hours at the wheel of the little Peugeot 203 station wagon I had just bought. It was my first Peugeot, a make to which I have remained faithful, as did many settlers before the invasion of Japanese cars.

For a long time we had no telephones. In urgent cases, one sent for a messenger, who came with a small forked stick; one wedged the carefully folded message into the fork, and the messenger dashed off as fast as his legs could carry him. It was a system that worked perfectly, though in practice there were few emergencies that called for it. The majority of illnesses in the area were similar to those seen in Europe. At this high, rarefied altitude pneumonia, influenza, rheumatism and sometimes a case of tuberculosis (TB) were the commonest complaints. It was only later, when I became a flying doctor, that I had to deal with tropical diseases.

There was no clinic nearby to which patients could be sent. When a villager became seriously ill, the family built him a little shelter of leaves and branches away from the family hut, and there was always someone about to feed and care for the patient. It was a sound practice, especially in cases of contagious disease, though I doubt if it was inspired by reasons of hygiene so much as by a strong belief in tribal magic. This method of dealing with the sick was similar to that practised by the Kikuyu. Should someone die in their hut, the family immediately moved away. The ridgepole of a hut is supported by a central post that unites the beams. It is a simple matter to dig up the ridgepole and bring the whole roof crashing down. Anyone seeing such a heap of rubble knows a body is buried under it.

Soon after my arrival at Ol Kalou, I came across one of these huts, hidden in the middle of a tangle of thorn bushes, with a skeleton under the debris. Njugana, my headman, who was with me, said, "An old man died here. That's why they pulled the hut down."

"Wouldn't it be wiser to reuse the building materials?"

"No, it would be bad, very very bad."

Valiant as my car was, there were places she simply could not reach, especially when the tracks were rain-soaked. Often there were no tracks at all—which gave me an opportunity to renew my passion for horses, a family tradition. My father was a fine horseman, and I had learned to ride in England when I was very young. At first, I hired a mount to make my visits; then I bought a horse of my own, and then several others, so I had to build loose-boxes and eventually found myself the owner of a small riding stable.

Mary Patten gave me grazing rights over a hundred and seventy acres of her farm, so their feeding cost me nothing, and finding grooms was no problem. You did not have to be rich in the Kenya of that time to lead what would have been a princely lifestyle in Europe. At weekends teams of local farmers played polo or hunted with their neighbours. Everyone, in typical British fashion, was keen on every kind of sporting activity.

The club at Ol Kalou was also very "pukka." This was the venue for "bashes" and dinner parties. We had a small movie theatre in which we ran a weekly film program. As I had lived and been mainly educated in England I felt completely at home in this thoroughly British setting. We were very well organized. John Harris, who lived at Subukia, was Master of the Hunt. His pack was made up of crossbreeds—beagles crossed with fox-hounds—who were perfectly adapted to the thick scrub over which we hunted. We wore hunting green, and the meet was at Thomson's Falls. As a member of the committee, it was my job to liaise with the many Afrikaans farmers in and around Ol Kalou. It was important to be on good terms with them because we had to ride over their land. These farmers were extremely religious and observed the Sabbath scrupulously. They strenuously objected to any form of exercise or sport on the Lord's day, and did their hunting on Saturdays.

Between us, we saddled about thirty steeds. The Field Master, a Dr. Bowles, and I always carried out first-aid kits. Falls and broken limbs were fairly common occurrences, since we had to contend with burrows, anthills and holes made by anteaters, into which the horses stumbled. My horses, trained on the polo field, were both wise and nimble, and generally managed to avoid pitfalls, though there were times when I, like everyone else, had to take a tumble. Occasionally, we had to jump obstacles. We had trouble with barbed-wire fences, which were really too dangerous to jump, though certain farmers who were excellent horsemen had taught their horses to jump close to fence posts from which they could gauge the height of the wire.

We hunted reedbuck, a species of little roe deer with prominent antlers. The rule was to hunt a single male, who often gave us the slip. Chased by the pack, the cunning little beast would take refuge in a thicket, being instantly replaced by one of his fellow deer who, in fine form, would dash off with the hounds in full cry after him. This kind of relay system took us on interminable cross-country rides, which, of course, added spice to the hunt. We rarely killed, though from time to time a buck had to be sacrificed to keep the hounds motivated. Sometimes their barking suddenly changed to a frenzied chorus, which told us that they had flushed out and shot off in furious pursuit of a jackal, an animal for which they seemed to have a particular enmity, member of the dog family though it is. Perhaps dogs, like people, sometimes hate their relatives. Very often the hounds lost their quarry, for jackals are adept at slipping into tiny crevices and lying doggo until danger is past.

The hunting season opened in December after the harvest and closed when sowing began in April. Our weekends were then dedicated to polo, which I played at the three clubs in our district, at Ol Kalou, Thomson's Falls and Gilgil. This annual program kept our horses active and in good condition, so that even in the rainy season I was able to visit my patients on the farms and villages on horseback, which would have been impossibile by car.

Another activity—scouting, which I had already practised enthusiastically in Mulhouse—took up a lot of my time. Almost as soon as I arrived I founded Ol Kalou's first troop of Girl Guides, while I, with my male dresser (nursing assistant), became leader of the Scouts. I organized camps on my farm, bringing together young people from the farms and schools, as well as the Asian children of local shopkeepers and the vicar's children. I got brilliant results from this lively, multiplying troop, though I was obliged to modify some of the tests in the Scouts' Manual to comply with local conditions. The Africans thought that to light a fire with matches was a big joke, so I made this test more interesting and imaginative. As a child, my dresser had been a shepherd in the Aberdares, and he knew how to make a fire by the most primitive method of all, twirling a small piece of hardwood in a depression in a piece of softwood until he produced a spark, with which he then set a tiny heap of brushwood alight. He taught us how to do this, and this soon became the troop's favourite test; we organized competitions between patrols to see which could light a bonfire fastest.

I expected my scouts to identify plants and trees and their various uses. The young Africans excelled at this. Even those who lived in towns or far from their original homeland could identify plants that cured diarrhoea or headaches, and they knew exactly how to build a hut. Their closeness to nature was astonishing. Map reading was another skill at which they seemed to be innately expert. The Mau Mau Emergency had not slowed down our normal activities and, as a member of the Police Reserve I had detailed maps of the area. The Africans had no difficulty in reading them, and had great fun in doing so. An African can draw you a detailed plan of his district in the sand without ever having looked at a map.

With the return of peace an Indian shopkeeper who traded in army surplus made me a handsome present of army tents. This enabled each Scout patrol to have their own tent, which they put up when they made camp. One of our more memorable camping trips took place on the shores of Lake Naivasha. We hiked round the Longonot volcano where we ran into a detachment of the famous Scottish Black Watch, who serenaded us with bagpipes. Night was falling and the summit of the volcano was crowned with mist. It was a magnificent sight. Another memorable expedition was our trip to Nyeri in 1957 to celebrate Baden-Powell's hundredth anniversary. We filed past his tomb in company with scouts from all over the world who had come to honour the memory of the founder of the Scout movement.

I don't regret having given so much of my time and energy to the Scouts. Thanks to this involvement I was able to mix with, and to understand the motivations of, the young members of the various groups in the community. This was not always possible under a colonial regime. I also taught my scouts the rudiments of health and hygiene and gave them first-aid courses at the end of which I presented them with a badge. But most importantly, I think I made it possible for these youngsters to escape the anxieties and pressures of a troubled time that offered an uncertain future. For my scouts, my farm was a little Eden in which they could give free rein to their high spirits, cut down trees, build scaffolding and make huts, activities the majority of other farmers would not have encouraged on their property.

By today's standards, the Scout movement may seem old-fashioned, but I still believe it is an admirable training school for encouraging initiative and courage. I have known of a number of examples of successful scout training. One of our girl guides, a patrol leader, lived in a small Kikuyu village that was attacked by the Mau Mau. Her mother was severely wounded by a bullet from a rifle pushed through the door. The girl did not panic; she kept calm, managed to escape from the house and ran through the bush to get help. Thanks to her coolness and initiative, her mother's life was saved.

After Independence, when I had to leave Ol Kalou, it was no longer possible for me to carry on work with my scouts, but the Africans took over and the Scout movement is still very much alive. From time to time I have the joy of meeting men and women who were in my troop and who remember those days with pleasure tinged with nostalgia.

The revolt of the Mau Mau, which had been simmering for years, burst into flame in 1952 and after the murder of Chief Waruhiu, a state of emergency was proclaimed. Kenyatta, leader of the Nationalist party, and five of his associates were accused of inciting the revolt, an accusation they hotly denied. They were condemned to seven years' forced labour and deported north to Lodwar, near Lake Turkana.

Almost immediately an underground movement sprang into being. Groups of rebels sprouted in the Aberdares and on Mount Kenya. Fifteen thousand fighters emerged from the forests to harass police stations, loyal villages and the farms of the white settlers. The great Mau Mau offensive lasted from March 1953 to the end of 1954. The rebels' greatest victory was the raid on the Naivasha police station that took place on 26 March 1953. The British mobilized fifty thousand men to fight the Mau Mau in their forest hideouts. The main victims of the rebels were members of their own tribe, other Kikuyu who remained loyal to the colonial government or who wanted to remain neutral. The rebels revived the binding of "blood oath" called *Muma* which may have been distorted into "Mau Mau," the name given them by the British. Nobody seems to be quite certain of the origin of this word, and the rebels called themselves "freedom fighters." They operated in small groups by night, hiding in the scrub and in the mountains by day. They did not attack towns or other tribes. Their main thrust was in the Aberdare mountains, which meant that we, living at Ol Kalou, were right in the thick of it.

The British eventually won this guerrilla war by using the same tactics as their adversaries. Not being as well equipped as the Americans in Vietnam served them in good stead, for it led them to adopt tactics that were eminently successful. At first they sent out patrols of six regular soldiers; later they used volunteers—ex-rebels and loyal Kikuyu from the police led by white settlers with blackened faces. Their aim was to infiltrate the Mau Mau camps as fellow terrorists.

It was a tough war, fought out in the bush and jungle in temperatures ranging from lowland tropical heat to the icy cold of the high altitudes. In Kenya, the forested lower slopes give way to high, dense, almost impenetrable clumps of bamboo which have to be hacked down to make a pathway. Or, if the climber is lucky, he may find a track made by some large animal. Above 10,000 feet is a kind of moor covered with heather and giant lobelias up to twelve feet high. It was difficult to spot the Mau Mau camps in this environment, far simpler to intercept Kikuyu sympathizers toiling up the mountain, carrying fresh supplies to the camps.

Ultimately, the British managed to flush out and destroy the most important Mau Mau bases, and in 1954 they captured the charismatic and popular Kikuyu leader General China. They then regrouped the rural population in strategic villages, and finally in 1954 they launched Operation Anvil. This was a monumental round-up of suspects in Nairobi, during which 100,000 people were arrested. The aim of this manoeuvre was to stop Mau Mau sympathizers in the capital and in the villages from supplying the underground. The terrorists could not survive without this vital lifeline. On 7 October 1956, volunteers in the Aberdare mountains tracked down, wounded and captured Dedan Kimathi, last of the Mau Mau leaders. He was tried and hanged.

The State of Emergency remained in force until the end of 1958. The war cost the lives of 32 European, 1,819 African and 26 Asian civilians killed by the Mau Mau, while it is estimated that the Army and Police lost 63 Europeans, 12 Asians and 101 Africans. Eleven and a half thousand Mau Mau freedom fighters died, of whom a thousand were hanged. From a purely military point of view the Mau Mau revolt was a failure, but its effect was far-reaching. It had set off a train of reforms, and nothing would ever be the same again. The inevitable end of this bloody affair was to be independence.

As a French woman living in Africa, I was not party to the subtleties of British policy in regard to their colonies, but I soon learned the reasoning behind the accusations the Kikuyu levelled at the white settlers. As peasant farmers the Kikuyu needed more land than that allocated to them, for in just half a century their numbers had swelled from 50,000 to over a million. They accused the Europeans of having stolen their land. The settlers argued that when they arrived in Kenya the disputed land was not under cultivation, and was used mainly as a thoroughfare by the nomadic Masai, who later agreed to move south to an area near Narok where they said the land suited them better. There was, therefore, a complete misunderstanding between the white settlers and the Kikuyu, which was greatly aggravated by their tribal custom of the ritual circumcision of girls. Colonial government had always disapproved of this practice and hoped that with the help of an educational program it might eventually cease. In 1951 a missionary of the Church of Scotland had reopened the dispute by denouncing the custom of excision. The Kikuyu chiefs reacted violently to this intrusion into their affairs.

Once again, disaster might have been averted had the proper channels of communication been opened between the two communities, and if black and white children had been able to talk to one another. As it was, white children were not required to learn Swahili. It is true that in 1900 white settlers arrived to find vast tracts of uncultivated land; they believed it belonged to nobody and was therefore up for grabs. No one had told them that epidemics of plague and smallpox had decimated the populations of these lands, nor did anyone inform them that the Kikuyu considered the region sacred and that it belonged to their ancestors. Again, there was no meaningful communication between Europeans and Africans, whose hatred of the intruders who had stolen their land continued to poison relations between the two races. Chiefs like Kenyatta and Kaggia, who were well-educated men, built on this hatred of the Europeans to form an organization to fight them.

I myself looked after both Europeans and Kikuyu. It was not up to me to take sides—that is, until the sad day when I had to defend my life and property. This is the classic chain of events where terrorist action is involved. Attacks provoke repression, which in turn redoubles the violence. It is difficult to remain neutral when one is a sitting target in the midst of disputed territory. I therefore had no option but to, like my friends, enrol in the volunteer force, while at the same time continuing my work as a doctor.

Early in 1952, a series of strange events occurred. Farm workers, having received mysterious messages, would flee and the following morning white farmers would find their livestock in the fields dead or with severed Achilles tendons.

The arrest of Kenyatta brought matters to a head. He was accused of being a "leader to darkness and death." From then on we were forbidden to sleep on our farms. We had to gather in the vicarage at Ol Kalou. Every evening at six o'clock, once surgery was over, I went to the vicarage. Guards were posted on our farms.

In other areas larger properties became rallying points and meeting places, and dormitories were arranged. This phase, which was far from comfortable, lasted for about three months. As soon as the authorities were persuaded that our lives were not threatened by hordes of spear-waving terrorists pouring down from the mountains, we were allowed to return to our homes and to be responsible for our own security. From then on we barricaded ourselves in our farms. We lit roaring fires to prevent the enemy from coming down the chimney. All doors were locked or bolted, and we kept the keys, as a number of people had been murdered by Mau Mau who had forced their servants to hand over the keys or to let them in. As further precautions, a heavy piece of furniture was pushed up against the door, and we dined with our pistols on the table close at hand.

The situation would have been far worse had the Mau Mau been equipped with modern weapons, but fortunately, theirs was an autonomous movement unsupported by any foreign power. The terrorists who attacked the farms, though high on hashish, were armed only with *pangas* (machetes). Their few crude firearms were made by local craftsmen and were as dangerous for the marksman as for his target. Our group patrolled in uniform on our polo ponies. In those days I never moved without my big .38 service revolver.

Sometimes I had to go to Nairobi. Returning, I would leave around eleven at night, knowing that there was no danger of being ambushed as the terrorists would never expect any road traffic at that late hour. One night, as I was driving down the old escarpment road towards Naivasha, I saw clouds of smoke rolling down the hillside and I had a dreadful premonition. With my revolver on my knee I drove on at full speed past Naivasha, where I felt the same strange foreboding.

On arriving at Ol Kalou, I was told that a massacre had taken place at Lari, and that the clouds of smoke I had seen came from the burning village. The Mau Mau had attacked a community of Christian Kikuyu (Baptists attached to Kijabe Mission) who, revolted by the initiation rites, had refused to take the Mau Mau oath. And my premonition had been right: at the very moment I was bypassing Naivasha the rebels were mounting a full-scale attack on the police station there. So twice that night I had come very close to real danger.

We lived in a state of permanent alarm but we were not really at war. We even managed to hunt in the middle of rebel territory. The revolt was confined to Kikuyu country and did not spread to the rest of Kenya, as the terrorists had hoped it might. The other main tribes, the Masai and the Samburu, refused to have anything to do with the Mau Mau, and many of them fought side by side with the British. The hotels in Nairobi were full, and to the south Henry King was filming Hemingway's novel *The Snows of Kilimanjaro* starring Ava Gardner, Susan Hayward and Gregory Peck. There were also a few fringe benefits accruing from the State of Emergency. For strategic reasons the authorities decided to build a splendid new road between Subukia and Ol Kalou, so we no longer had to go the long way round via Nakuru. This was one dark cloud with a silver lining.

During this traumatic period, my brother François came out to stay with me. One evening we left Nairobi by car but after two hours on the road I realized the petrol gauge was getting alarmingly low. In my hurry to get back to Ol Kalou, I had made the grave mistake of forgetting to fill up. We were not too far from our destination, but we might well come to a stop at any moment in dangerous country. When the car finally did stop, I turned to my puzzled brother and said, "We had better stay on the road.

It's less dangerous. There's a farm nearby belonging to friends. They will lend us a can of petrol." With which I handed him my revolver and walked off into the bush. François will freely admit now that he was far from happy as he stood by the car, revolver at the ready, waiting for me to come back. When one thinks danger is near, the slightest sound in the stillness of the African night assumes an alarming significance.

At this time there were a hundred thousand Europeans living in Kenya. As has been mentioned, there were few European fatalities, from the Mau Mau revolt, though a number of people were wounded in shooting accidents. All adult civilians were armed. Those who enrolled in the Police Reserve were not fully trained, however, and quite a few bullets found the wrong target—I had a good many opportunities to complete my training in traumatology.

At five o'clock one morning a sergeant knocked at my door: "Come at once, doctor. There has been a very serious accident."

Grabbing my first-aid kit, I followed him to his car. We drove ten miles at great speed to where a military truck was precariously balanced over a precipice. Half the driver's head had been shot away at point-blank range and there was nothing I could do for him.

The tragedy had begun in the most mundane way. The patrol had spent the night in ambush. At dawn, a truck came to pick them up and take them back to their camp. Before boarding the truck the sergeant should have checked that all rifles were unloaded, but for once this elementary precaution was not observed. One of the soldiers was sitting behind the driver on the spare wheel leaning on his rifle. Perhaps he accidentally pulled the trigger when the truck went over a bump. Anyhow, the shot blew the driver's head off. The sergeant, sitting next to him, was able to turn off the ignition and stop them rolling into the ravine below. My role was limited to certifying death and giving tranquillizers to both the sergeant, who felt responsible for the accident, and the soldier, who had collapsed.

A year later a police officer at Ol Kalou asked me for a detailed report of this affair. The military police had strenuously pursued their investigations and had asked the civilian police for assistance. Some keen amateur sleuths had discovered that the soldier who had fired the fateful shot and the victim had the same girlfriend, and this, the police thought, might well have been a motive for murder. This seemed to me not only absurd but also impossible. If the soldier in question had really wanted to dispose of his rival he would certainly have found other, less public opportunities to kill him rather than in full view of the entire patrol travelling in a moving truck, which might well have overturned and killed him as well as his victim. My statement was accepted, and I heard no more of this sad incident.

Returning home one evening I found a lieutenant, in uniform, lying flat on his face on my sofa. He had been leading a reconnaissance column when he was shot accidentally in the buttocks by the soldier behind him carrying a Patchett sub-machine gun. He was in great pain, and was deeply humiliated at receiving a wound in such an unromantic place. The wound was superficial, and having given him first aid, I took him to the hospital at Nakuru.

On another occasion I was called out in the middle of the night. I was not really surprised, as I knew a big military operation was taking place in the Aberdares, which had been placed out of bounds to civilians for three days. At dusk a patrol of the K.P.R.—the Police Reserve—saw a column of smoke rising above the trees. From this smoke signal, the officer in command concluded that a band of freedom fighters were cooking their supper and he decided to attack them with five of his men. He should have known that the Mau Mau, highly trained in guerrilla tactics, would never make this sort of mistake, most members of the K.P.R. were farmers who had been issued with a uniform but did not have much military training.

The patrol creeping through the forest saw shadowy figures around a campfire and without more ado opened fire. One man, cooking potatoes, fell to the ground, and the others fled the K.P.R. patrol in hot pursuit. A few moments later an English voice rang out in the night with the standard challenge, "Halt! Who goes there?" and their pursuers stopped dead in their tracks. Their quarry were not terrorists: they were a detachment of rookies from the Gloucestershire Regiment. The only experienced soldier with them was their sergeant, just back from Korea, and it was he who had been wounded. He was brought down the mountain on a litter and I took him to the hospital at Nakuru where he was rushed into the operating theatre. The surgeons had to remove one of his kidneys and a piece of his liver but fortunately he soon recovered, to thank his lucky stars that the K.P.R. man who had wounded him was not a very good shot. It was also lucky that the real soldiers did not instantly open fire without further investigation, as their weapons were much more powerful than the little Patchetts used by the farmers.

Apart from these military interludes I continued to visit my patients at night, but the absence of telephones on the farms made my life extremely complicated. The farmers used to fetch me in their own cars, perhaps because a small daughter had been taken ill or a wife was going into labour. When I got to the patient I often found that there was no emergency, and once I had assessed and dealt with the situation I wanted to go home again as quickly as possible, and naturally I expected the farmer to drive me back. But they always found excuses to delay me and to keep me there on the farm as long as possible. They wanted the doctor to stay overnight and I was their prisoner, which did not suit me in the least. I soon found a way round this problem: thereafter, when a farmer came to fetch me I followed him back in my own car, and was then free to leave when I wanted to.

I never had any trouble when carrying out my nocturnal medical duties. The Mau Mau preferred to attack in the early evening when there were plenty of people around. I imagine that late at night they were in their camps, holding meetings or practising their unsavoury rites. I did, however, take security measures. I was always armed and escorted by two large dogs with reassuringly intimidating fangs.

My first dog was a bull terrier. I called him Winny because he bore an astonishing resemblance to Winston Churchill. He did not live long, dying of tick fever, which I had not then learned to look out for. The animal becomes anemic, with pallor of the gums, an enlarged spleen and a rapid pulse rate. Unless the illness is treated at once it can prove fatal. Bully, Winny's successor, was a Rhodesian ridgeback, so called for the ridge of hair growing the wrong way along their backs. In Rhodesia these courageous animals are trained to hunt lion. After Bully came his daughter Punch, then Buck, Judy and Suzy, last of his line. All my memories of Ol Kalou are inextricably bound up with my canine companions. They followed me everywhere, and often caused me extreme anxiety. They were dedicated hunters, a sport they found it all to easy to pursue in the environment in which we lived.

One morning Judy and Buck shot off into the trees. They stayed away all day and I waited up for them all night. The next day I decided to go and look for them on horseback in the pouring rain. I rode from farm to farm and from village to village asking if anyone had seen my dogs. After several hours, drenched and exhausted, I was on my way back through the forest when I heard the sound of loud barking. This led me to my beauties still madly pursuing the wild boar that had been the reason for their hurried departure from home. These beasts were their favourite prey, although Buck had already lost a piece of his tail in an encounter with a bear that rounded on him, but even this serious brush with danger had not cured him.

I was very sad when I lost Judy. I was travelling by car with my father and friends through a desert region north of Nanyuki, when suddenly we came on a herd of giraffe running at full pelt. At this sight, Judy, wild with excitement jumped out of the window, breaking her lead as she did so, and chased after the herd. We waited for hours, scouring the place and calling her name, and later I came back many times to the spot to see if I could trace her, but I never found her, and even now when I fly over that particular spot, I always think of my poor lost Judy.

For Europeans who live in Africa the company of a dog is of vital importance. Our contact with civilization has so dulled our senses that we are now unable to read nature's signs and signals. Dogs have this art. They complement the senses we lack and are able to warn us of danger; they can scent a hostile animal and

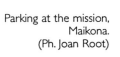

At the controls of
Alpha Zulu Tango.
(Ph. B. Desestres)

Parking at the mission,
Maikona.
(Ph. Joan Root)

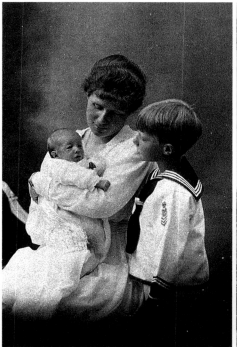

Top left:
François and Anne with their mother,
May 1918.
(Ph. Author)
Anne and Peggo, at Mulhouse in 1926.
(Ph. Author)

Top right:
Henry Spoerry at Ol Kalou in 1953.
(Ph. Author)

Bottom right:
Anne at two years of age.
(Ph. Author)

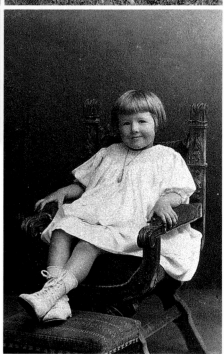

Top left:
Ol Kalou in 1952. (Ph. Author)

Bottom left:
Anne and her team at the
hospital in Aden in 1949.
(Ph. Author.)

Top right:
Anne on 'Sinbad' during the emergency.
(Ph. Author.)

Bottom right:
Anne and her trainer, Francis, at the Ol Kalou.
(Ph. Author.)

Top left and centre left:
Loyangalani, a fishing village in El Molo.
(Ph. B. Desestres)

Bottom left:
Merille: Rendille children. (Ph. J. Root)

Top right:
Loyangalani, with a Turkana family.
(Ph. B. Desestres)

Bottom right:
Loyangalani, women making "changaa," a beer
made from corn.
(Ph. B. Desestres)

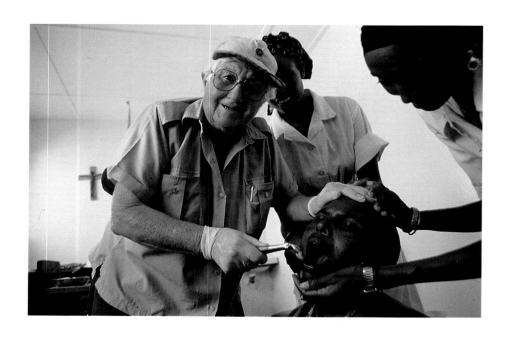

Above and below:
Examinations at the missions in Marsabit district.
(Ph. B. Desestres)

Above:
Examining a woman's ear in Turkana.
(Ph. Sylvie Maubec)

Below:
In Ileret, attending to a patient at the airstrip.
(Ph. S. Maubec)

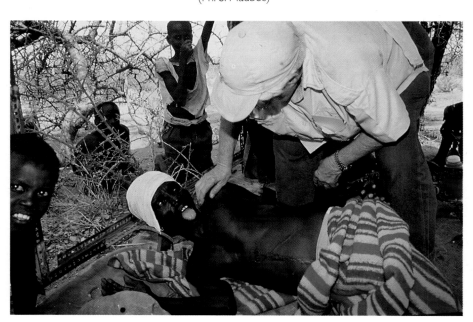

Top left:
Flying above Paradise Lake in Marsabit
(Ph. B. Desestres)

Bottom left:
Anne in the glider.
(Ph. B. Desestres)

Top right:
Illeret, at the edge of Lake Turkana.
(Ph. B. Desestres)

Lower right:
Approaching Nairobi.
(Ph. B. Desestres)

Above:
Michael Wood arrives at his farm in Ol Molog. (Ph. AMREF/A. Edgeworth).

Below:
The "Flying Doctors" pilots (1965) with Anne Spoerry and Michael Wood.
(Ph. AMREF)

Above:
Anne Spoerry in her office at Wilson Airport. (Ph. S. Maubec)
Below:
Sir Michael Wood operating in Loliondo, Tanzania, 1983.
(Ph. AMREF/ G. Backhurst).

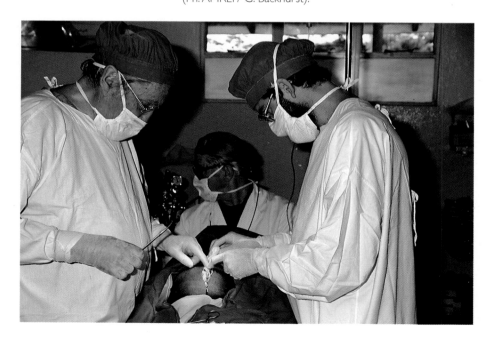

Above, top right and bottom right:
At the clinic in the North, Anne meets with the patients
and nurses. (Ph. S. Maubec and B. Desestres).

Below:
Lodwar, Turkana (Ph. Joan Root).

Above: Delivering vaccines to the clinic at Lamu.
(Ph. B. Desestres)
Centre: In the streets of Lamu.
(Ph. S. Maubec)
Below: Distributing food at the refugee camp in Walda
(Ph. S. Maubec)

Above: Relaxing on the weekend, Subukia
(Ph. S. Maubec)

Centre: Milking cows at Subukia
(Ph. S. Maubec)

Below: Anne in her favourite position
at the farm in Subukia.
(Ph. S. Maubec)

Above and below:
The pleasure of farming, Subukia. (Ph. S. Maubec)

can keep it at a distance or, more simply, they can help us find our way when we have lost our markers.

If the truth be told I became the owner of Lokolwa farm in Ol Kalou rather under duress. The property I leased was part of a 1,000-acre farm owned by Mary Patten, who kept 150 acres for her own use and leased the rest to a farmer, Plater, who hailed from the Tyrol. He had apparently been an excellent soldier in the Wehrmacht in the First World War, but I must confess we did not get on very well together. In 1959, when Mary Patten died, her godson, who was her heir, discussed the future of the farm with me. He told me that Plater wanted to take over the whole property, which would, of course, have deprived me of the hundred and fifty acres I rented for my horses.

"Your best solution," the new owner said, "is to buy the whole property outright. Plater will then be forced to leave, as he hasn't sufficient cash to buy the property."

I realized that the heir was pressuring me a little, not to say blackmailing me, but I also knew that even if I had to pay a bit over the odds to acquire it, I would be free to keep the farm, to which I had become very attached.

I never regretted my decision. Farming was in my blood. Father had demonstrated his agricultural ability during the war when he provided his family and friends with home-grown produce at Cavalaire. On the other hand, I was a bit shaken to discover that I was the owner of a fairly large enterprise, and my self-confidence ebbed to zero when I realized I was a farmer with no farming equipment. Luckily, good neighbours came to my rescue and steered me in the right direction.

"It's simple," Nevil Griffin said reassuringly. "For starters you'll need a tractor, plough and harrow."

The last of these he sold me for forty shillings and I still have it. I found a little Massey-Ferguson tractor and trailer at a sale, which cost me £150. I then bought a plough and put it in the trailer. I found a young lad to drive the tractor and followed him in my car, feeling very proud and every inch the real farmer. The Massey-Ferguson is still in use at Subukia.

Farming in the Kenya highlands is very much like farming in Europe, though at an altitude of 8,000 feet growth is slow and one cannot, as in the warmer lowlands, hope for two harvests a year. Admittedly, I only farmed 120 to 150 of the 1,000 acres I owned and left the rest as forest and pasture land. Cereals were sown in March or April during the rainy season. The corn and barley harvests were brought in between November and Christmas, as were oats for animal feed. Besides my horses, I had milk cows, beef cattle and four hundred sheep, sheared annually in July. I once tried pig farming, but soon gave it up as it was not profitable. I had fifteen acres under pyrethrum, a white-flowered member of the chrysanthemum family, whose powdered heads produce an insecticide. Although there are constant developments in the chemical field, pyrethrum remains one of Kenya's most important natural resources.

In spite of a favourable climate tempered by the altitude and good volcanic soil, farming on the Equator is never simple. Through the years we have had appalling droughts and equally devastating floods. For eight years Lake Nakuru was bone-dry, an immense stretch of white soda ash heated during the summer months, by eddies of warm air and swirled upwards in great clouds that fell on the neighbouring town and nearby fields. In 1961 the lake filled up again. The Masai, who had once lived in this region, said that according to their ancestors even Lake Naivasha had once been completely dried out. Farming in such a capricious climate was not the easiest way of making a fortune. Few people achieved this, and I was not one of them. Yet in spite of all the difficulties I loved my life as a farmer, and would never have given it up had events not decided otherwise.

Since 1956 Kenya had been in the throes of violent political agitation with numerous factions jockeying for supremacy. Both Europeans and Africans were involved, but the country remained calm, and life seemed to be functioning normally. The price of land was sky-high, which proved that the settlers had every confidence in the future. I shared their optimism by paying £10,000 for my farm, which in 1956 was a large sum of money.

In 1960 the Lancaster House Conference came like a thunder-bolt out of a clear blue sky. The European settlers became aware that Her Majesty's government was not biased in their favour and that Independence—Uhuru—was inexorably on the way. Kenyatta was moved from a prison cell to more comfortable quarters in a house at Lodwar in the north, and on 1 August 1961 the Governor, Sir Patrick Renison, granted him his freedom so as to enable him to take part in the progress to independence in Kenya.

From that moment events moved very fast. Owing to his prestige Kenyatta succeeded in uniting the various African factions. His own party, KANU (Kenya African National Union), won the legislative elections in 1963 and on the second of June Kenyatta became the first Prime Minister of Kenya; Independence was proclaimed on 12 December 1963, twenty-four months after Tanganyika and fifteen months after Uganda. Britain's colonial empire in Africa had ceased to exist.

Kenyatta, well aware of the effect a mass white exodus would have on the economic stability of the country, did his utmost to reassure the European farmers that their rights would be respect-ed. In this he was not altogether successful and many settlers left for South Africa, Rhodesia, Australia and New Zealand, though quite a number eventually returned. First to leave were the South Africans, who had good reason to be apprehensive about their future in a country with an African government.

I met Kenyatta at Ol Kalou when he was prime minister. He had called a meeting of white settlers to explain and clarify his policy that those who wished to remain were welcome to do so. That he meant what he said was apparent since he was keeping the Russians and the Chinese at a distance and had never shown the slightest interest in Communism, a stand that was to be of some benefit to Kenya. Kenyatta was a very shrewd politician and the Europeans trusted him. He had lived for many years in Britain, where he had married an Englishwoman. He was able to control the extremists who wanted to grab everything immedi-ately, and he made certain of maintaining good relations with London, since Kenya was economically dependent on Great

Britain, which provided the loans to finance the purchase of land from the settlers—land which was then redistributed to African farmers. Equally, the compensation paid out to expropriated white settlers also came from London.

I was one of those obliged to sell their property to the new government. Ol Kalou was part of the "Million Acre" scheme under which all the big farms in the area—one of the most fertile and productive in the country—were divided into fifty-acre plots and given to Africans with some knowledge of agriculture and farming. I received adequate compensation for the loss of my property and the regime seemed to be working satisfactorily.

I was the last European to leave Ol Kalou. For a year after my farm was sold I went on living there. Gradually my friends and neighbours left, and with them, of course, went my livelihood as a doctor. I was back to square one, on the lookout for a post in the government service—there was never any question of my leaving Kenya.

The departure of the white settlers left a great gap. Previously, in cases of childbirth or other serious illness, the settlers had made their own arrangements to transport their family or staff to hospital. A new service was needed to carry out this task, particularly as the British doctors who administered the service had also left.

The new district of Nyandarua had been created in our area. Those in charge of it were looking for a medical officer, as the nearest hospital was some distance away, at Thomson's Falls. I accepted this post and signed a two-year contract. Nobody gave any thought to the fact that the workload might be too heavy for a woman: at that time the Administration did not have much choice. I found myself facing a gigantic task. My district extended over sixty miles to the south of the Aberdares and the whole medical infrastructure had to be reconstituted from scratch. On a meagre budget I had to find buildings that could be converted into dispensaries and somehow staff them.

I found a temporary solution to the problem that worked out well and, in the event, lasted for some time. I bought two second-hand Land-Rovers and had them completely reconditioned—after the farmers' exodus there were a lot of these around. Manned by a crew consisting of a driver and a clinical officer, each Land-Rover had its own round, visiting five communities twice weekly. This provided a fixed, regular medical presence in ten different parts of the district. The Land-Rovers also carried boxes of medicines and folding tables (also army surplus) for use during the clinics, and at night they did duty as ambulances in cases of emergency. At each stop we had made arrangements with a school or a shop to receive our patients. This system worked reliably all year round, and I believe my superiors were happy with it—they were certainly getting value for their money.

During the two years I worked out my government contract I also had to find somewhere to live, now that I had lost Ol Kalou. This was not easy as I was on the road much of the time, but a plan was forming in my mind. I was learning to fly at a little airfield at Subukia, thirty miles north of Ol Kalou. Feeling that I was beginning what was to be a long love affair with flying, I wanted to be as close as possible to the airfield. Eventually I found a small farm at Subukia itself. The old colonel who had rented the property had just died and his widow wanted to return to Europe. The owner was prepared to sell, providing he was paid in England. This presented no problem and in a short time the farm was mine. After Independence land values had fallen steeply and I spent far more on redecorating and getting the whole place the way I wanted it than I paid for the property itself. Thirty years later I have no regrets over what was, after all, only a minor extravagance. On the contrary, my only regret is that although Subukia is my official home I only have time to spend my weekends there.

At Subukia I have twenty-five acres of good land and some fine trees. Two little rivers that never dry up flow through my fields. We are in a valley at a lower altitude than Ol Kalou and therefore a little warmer. We are on the Equator but the climate is mild all year round. In order to fence my property I managed to salvage the cedar posts I'd had at Ol Kalou. I knew their value, as they do not rot and are termite-proof. My house is a bungalow built of volcanic stone that has all but disappeared under a curtain of flowering creeper. The house sits in a frame of very large trees, home to a flock of silver-cheeked hornbills. There is a living room, a big bedroom and three smaller rooms. The house is filled with books and pictures and all the memorabilia of my forty-five years in Africa. We have no electricity, and at night we pump up the old Tilley lamps, which run on paraffin and compressed air. Hot water for the bathroom comes from a metal tank in the courtyard heated by a wood fire.

For the uninitiated, a night in Subukia cannot be said to induce peaceful slumber. Nature is at her noisiest. The most alarming noises are the cries of the tree hyraxes. This small animal, about the size of a rabbit, is developmentally a close relative of the elephant, and makes an appalling din. First a noise like the creaking of an old door, then agonized shrieks, ending with a pitiful childlike wail. It sounds for all the world like the soundtrack of a horror film.

This reminds me of the story of the Italian officer prisoners of war who climbed Mount Kenya. When the British reconquered Ethiopia in 1941 they took a number of Italian prisoners and sent them to Kenya. The NCOs were sent to work on the farms, where they had comparative freedom, but the officers were confined to a camp at Nanyuki at the foot of Mount Kenya. Bored stiff, three of the young officers, all experienced Alpinists, decided to climb the huge sombre mass towering above them, which seemed to offer a challenge to their mountaineering skills. They managed to obtain some clothing and equipment, as well as a few provisions. They then slipped out of the camp, which was not well guarded as the guards well knew their prisoners had little interest in escaping into the unknown terrors of the surrounding bush.

The three escapers had no maps, only an illustration of Mount Kenya on the label off a tin of condensed milk. They toiled up the steep mountain slope, making their way up a glacier that led them to Point Lenana at an altitude of 16,325 feet. There they planted an Italian flag and scrambled down. It was a courageous and praiseworthy exploit, carried out with brio and a minimum of equipment. Hungry and exhausted, they managed to creep back into the camp without being seen, and their fellow officers hid them for days to give them time to rest and recover their strength. As soon as they were fit again they owned up to the British C.O. of the camp, who was not at all amused by their exploits and had them locked up.

Brave as these officers were, they said afterwards when recounting their adventure that, on the first night of their climb they were terrified by the noises made by the hyraxes and were certain that a bloody fight was going on nearby, in which they were likely to be caught up. It took them some time to realize that all these ghastly noises were only made by small animals.

Around the house and outbuildings at Subukia can be heard a veritable orchestra of farmyard noises. Chickens, turkeys and geese are allowed to roam at will; I also keep rabbits and sheep, and a few cows graze in the neighbouring fields. My kitchen garden, laid out between the two streams, provides the kitchen with fresh salads, cabbages, carrots and a cornucopia of other succulent vegetables. It is bliss to know that you can grow anything all the year round. I also cultivate three hundred coffee trees and grow enough maize to feed both staff and cattle. All this local produce is invaluable to the small community around me, for a dozen families live and work on my farm.

Very probably the farm costs me more than it brings in, but that is really not a problem. This is the lifestyle I have chosen and I would not want to live any other way. Not that I want to copy Marie Antoinette's charming pretence at farming at the Petit Trianon: at Subukia I am responsible for the welfare of quite a number of people. Most of my staff have been with me for a very long time: Njuguna, my farm manager, began working for me in 1953; the others were taken on around 1964—some thirty years ago. The original group had children who have grown up and had their own children, and all of these I have put through school.

As the only practising doctor for miles around, my weekends are fully occupied. AMREF's radio link keeps me in touch with the Foundation, and with other farmers in the district. We have regular scheduled times for going on the air, which gives us the opportunity of catching up with local news, such as accidents and cattle thefts, and enables us to alert those concerned.

I built a little clinic next to the house, with a thatched shelter serving as a waiting room. Mothers bring their children, so I am able to keep a close eye on the health of both the mother and child and on family planning. For contraception I use three-monthly injections of Depo-Provera. This product has enabled us to make progress in introducing family planning—having one of the world's highest birth rates is one of Kenya's most crucial problems. Four quarterly injections are sufficient for the effect to be prolonged for a further year. These hormone injections have several advantages: they are reliable; the women do not have to buy expensive packs of oral contraceptive pills or remember to take one every day; nor do they have to hide them away from husbands who do not agree with contraception. I have no idea where or how the anti-Depo-Provera campaign began, but the drug got a terrible press in the West, mainly in the United States, where it was accused of being dangerous to health and even of causing cancer, and this in spite of the millions of women who have used it without ill effects. I suspect that pharmaceutical competitors may have had something to do with the story.

Subukia was not included in the "Million Acre Scheme," and redistribution of land took place spontaneously as and when the European farmers left. Many had stayed on at first after Independence: they were young and their farms were doing well, and they liked the full social life—there were often as many as three hundred farmers and their wives at a party. But after the worldwide depression of 1973, the palmy days were over, and the farmers left one by one till the district was emptied of Europeans. Co-operatives stepped in and bought the deserted farms, parcelling out the land in five-acre plots to Africans. It was a bit of a lottery for the new landowners, for certain farms were fertile but others less so. This caused the same problems that faced us in France when the land redistribution operation took place. With its population growth of 4.3 percent a year, the demand for land is very great in Kenya, and pressures on the last big landowners are very strong.

The Kikuyu are an obstinate race who do not give up easily. They are even prepared to use a certain amount of intimidation to get what they want. For example, you might receive a letter from the local co-operative informing you that it has been decided to buy your farm. When you reply that you do not want to sell, they try another tactic. Without your knowledge they pay a sum of money into your bank account, then inform you that they are now the owners of your property! You protest vigorously: "But I haven't sold my farm."

"Yes, you have," they reply. "You have been paid, and you have even banked the money."

I myself have a very strict rule that no one can pay anything into my bank account without my signature. I know all the tricks, having learned a lot while trying to help my friend Rosemary to find a strip of farmland on which to survive.

Today Rosemary is nearly forty. I knew her first as a little girl handicapped by a virulent attack of polio. I looked after her and saw her through school, where she received her Primary Leaving Certificate. She then attended the Young Women's Christian Association of Limuru, where she learned dressmaking, first aid, and cookery. She then acquired a diploma that entitled her to teach other women. Rosemary never married, but she has two sons. I put the eldest, Peter, through college and then got him a post with AMREF, where he now works as an accounts assistant.

There are many single mothers among the Kikuyu. When their women manage to escape the pressures of tradition and obtain an education, they do not marry. They have received the message of what marriage involves, loud and clear. A Kikuyu wife has no rights: she is literally owned by her husband, who has complete jurisdiction over their children and control over her earnings. Many of the men are more interested in beer than hard work.

In the past, the traditional system worked smoothly. The men went hunting, or waged war against their neighbours, while the women kept the home fires burning, and saw to the children and to their domestic chores. The Kikuyu women of today are different. They have broken with tradition. They have had enough of male domination. Most are hard working and intelligent, and do not drink. More and more women nowadays take charge of their own destinies, living their lives to their own satisfaction and keeping their earnings for themselves. We are, I believe, watching the birth of a new matriarchal society.

Rosemary's mother belonged to a group of women who practised traditional Kikuyu dances. President Kenyatta loved these dances, and often invited this particular group to perform at his home on Lake Nakuru. In lieu of cash he presented them with farms, which they turned into a co-operative. Rosemary inherited one of these plots, but she had to fight tooth and nail to keep it. I supported her claim to ownership, but at that time there were no clear legal rights to property. A single woman is very vulnerable. In order to make Rosemary feel more secure I built her a little house so that the co-operative could not force her to move to a less desirable plot. She cultivated the plot and enclosed it—again, it is more difficult to repossess land under cultivation and into which the occupants have put money. Then Rosemary acquired some more fields nearby with her own money and she ended up with a nice little five-acre property on which she grows coffee. Her childhood polio left her able to work only with great difficulty and I am always touched by her amazing courage when I see her working in the fields despite her handicap, yet she always smiles and I have never heard her complain.

When one lives among the Africans there are many ways of helping them, particularly if one can find a means of improving their living conditions by simple means and at little cost. For example, I advise them to use baked-clay ovens to economize on fuel—wood is now scarce in Africa, and careless use of it is destroying the forests and allowing erosion of the hillsides. One of my main problems is the education of the teenagers on the farm. Secondary education in Kenya is not free. The government initiated the British system of cost-sharing, which has its merits, as people feel both involved and responsible when they have to pay for something. The down side to this philosophy, however, is that those who are poor cannot send their children to college unless they find a benefactor or sponsor. I support a lot of the farm's teenagers in this way. In exchange for my financial commitment I ask them to help out with the farm work. I also keep tabs on their progress, and if their reports are not up to scratch they get the rough side of my tongue.

Subukia may seem the end of the world, but thanks to my radio and plane I am not at all isolated. As an active member of the flying doctor service I am always completely mobile and ready for instant action.

On Sunday 1 August 1982, while listening on the AMREF frequency, I heard that a *coup d'état* was in progress in Nairobi. At dawn its inhabitants had woken to the sound of gunfire. The radio announced the overthrow of President Moi by the Council of National Redemption. The rebels were young officers and men, mostly Luos, in the Air force. The airport had been closed and they had taken over the Post Office and the radio and television station in the centre of town. The situation was grave. Looters from the shanty towns were on the rampage. Students had joined the rebels and there was fighting near the AMREF headquarters. Our director, Michael Wood, evacuated the staff and shut down the office, so I lost contact with Nairobi.

I continued to listen on our wavelength and the next day I picked up an urgent appeal issued by the Tom M'Boya Hospital on the island of Rusinga, in Lake Victoria. Two little girls had been attacked by a mad dog and their faces badly bitten. I knew this was a life-or-death emergency, for the rabies virus makes its way through the nerves to the brain, and when that distance is short, symptoms may appear very rapidly—it is far better to be bitten on the ankle than on the head. Rusinga is 125 miles west of Subukia. I was the only doctor available and by sheer good luck I had a supply of anti-rabies vaccine in my paraffin-powered fridge. Packing the vaccine in a thermal bag, I dashed off to my plane. As a state of emergency had just been proclaimed, officially no vehicles were allowed on the road, and all civilian aircraft were grounded.

I had a young French doctor, Jacques-Florian Letouneulx, who was also an excellent pilot, staying with me at the time. We agreed to disregard the ban and undertake this mission, come what might. We took off, taking care to avoid flying over the police station, and flew at a great height so as to make it impossible to identify our plane. We crossed the Mau escarpment at 10,000 feet, descending steeply over Lake Victoria on our way to Rusinga, taking an hour in all.

I made radio contact with the administrator of the hospital, and asked them to come and pick up the vaccine as quickly as possible as we were in a mighty hurry to get away. I flew over the landing strip to make sure it was free of cows, police cars or soldiers. It seemed deserted. We were met by an old man on a bicycle who told us he had been sent to take charge of the vaccine as the hospital car had broken down. This was no big deal, as the hospital was only a little over a mile away. As soon as the messenger had pedalled away, we took off, which was just as well, as a big storm was just about to break over Subukia, and we touched down just before it burst. I don't think the police ever found out about our clandestine mission—at least nobody ever mentioned it to me.

During our flight there was complete radio silence. Apparently, not a single aircraft was aloft in the whole country; on the AMREF waveband, however, I got a call from one of our stations in Tanzania. Our colleagues there had no knowledge of what was happening in Kenya and were in a panic because they were unable to make contact with the outside world. I told them what was going on and advised them to keep calm and to wait until the situation was resolved, which it was very quickly.

On the following day, I regained contact with AMREF. I was told I could fly to Wilson in the afternoon, providing I did not fly over the barracks, where fighting was still in progress. Instead, I flew over the national park where the giraffes were strolling about, completely indifferent to all the fuss.

Soon after landing, I hurried to the town, where all traces of the two days of looting and fighting had already been removed. At 6 p.m. President Moi announced over the radio that the revolt was over and that the ground forces had remained loyal and saved the government. During the revolt, the president had remained on his farm, near Nakuru, until a military convoy came to escort him back to Nairobi.

There are not many Europeans left in Subukia today. Those who stayed on are old. They are dear friends, with whom I remain in close contact. Some of them have led extraordinary lives and I never tire of hearing their stories.

Arthur Randall Swift was seventeen when he first came to Kenya to work on his uncle's farm at Thika, north of Nairobi. He had free keep, but his wages were minimal, and it took him a long time to save up enough money to buy a motorcycle. While awaiting mechanical transport he had to use shanks's pony and his prowess as a pedestrian earned him the name "Hobo." The nickname stuck, his real names were forgotten and I never heard his wife call him anything but Hobo.

During the second World War Swift served as a captain in the King's African Rifles. He fought in the Ethiopian campaign and said that, far from being "chocolate soldiers," the Italians were doughty fighters. Ethiopia was recaptured only after hard and bitter fighting on both sides. From Mogadishu, Swift crossed the desert and took part in the capture of Addis Ababa on 6 April, 1941. Fighting went on in the north, however, and in mid-May the Duke of Aosta, who commanded the Italian troops, tried to take refuge in the Amba-Alaghi massif, which rises to 10,000 feet. After a tough siege he was forced to capitulate with 7,000 men, but received full battle honours.

During the fighting, Swift received a bullet in the throat, which he miraculously survived. His war was over and he was evacuated to the Military Hospital at Nairobi, where he spent his convalescence. The Commander-in-Chief paid regular visits to the wards, stopping by each bed and delivering the same little speech. "How are you. I hope you are better."

On one occasion, Hobo was out of bed, standing to attention, with an elegant scarf over his bandages. The General looked him up and down muttering, "What on earth are you doing here?" He went on to the next bed. It was easy to read his mind, and to know what he was thinking of Hobo. "Who the heck is this chap, and why on earth isn't he in bed like the others?"

The whole ward was shocked. The beds were, in the main, occupied by patients suffering from diarrhoea or from minor injuries caused by falling off their bicycles. Hobo was the only officer in the ward to have been wounded by enemy action and was one of the heroes of the famous battle of Amba-Alaghi. The very next day the General came back to the ward to pay a special visit to Hobo to make up for his blunder.

After his apprenticeship with his uncle, Hobo managed several farms before being able to buy himself the property near Subukia. Over the years he became an expert cattle-breeder and a specialist in growing coffee. One year, however, probably from being overwhelmed with work, he pruned his coffee bushes rather late, and his friends and neighbours shook their heads and issued dire warnings that he had made a ghastly mistake. As it happened, unexpected rain meant Hobo was able to bring in one of his best coffee harvests that year. He was not particularly proud of this incident, and would tell it to illustrate that agriculture in Africa is a lottery, as poor Karen Blixen had discovered to her cost on her Ngong Hills farm.

Hobo liked to talk about his uncle, who he said was a splendid example of the mettlesome early white settlers in Kenya. In his youth this uncle had worked in a coffee and sisal plantation above Thika. He and one of his friends liked to go dancing at Nairobi's Muthaiga Club, which was thirty-five miles away over a badly rutted road. The two eager dancers had only one bicycle between them, and no other transport was available. Undaunted, the young men devised a rather clever solution. One of them would set out on foot, followed a bit later by the other on the bicycle. The cyclist would overtake the walker and carry on for a further ten minutes, then dismount, leave the bicycle by the side of the road, and start walking himself. In this way both young men reached the club and, after happily dancing the night away, return to work the next morning in the same manner.

Hobo owned a stable of magnificent horses. He was an accomplished horseman and his wife, Marian, was an expert in dressage. Hobo was a fine polo player, but his real hobby was painting, and when he retired this became one of his main sources of income. He painted wonderful landscapes of Kenya, many from just outside his own front door. Although he had lived here most of his adult life he never ceased to marvel at the amazing beauty of his adopted country. He was also passionate about every aspect of the world of nature. He loved animals, birds and plants and could identify any specimen brought for his opinion. Stretching away from his house his land was shaded by tall trees where troops of colobus monkeys played. These creatures have a distinctive black-and-white fur that makes them look as if they are wearing dinner jackets. Sadly, their beautiful pelts have brought them to the verge of extinction, for they were hunted by Europeans to make bedside rugs and by the Africans for ceremonial costumes. Even today colobus fur is used to adorn the shakos of the regimental band of the Kenya Rifles.

Hobo and I used to reminisce about the "old days" when there was a far greater abundance of fauna. At that time it was not unusual to see bushbuck, an antelope with twisted horns, and prowling hartwolf, a species of jackal. Elephant on the move were an ordinary sight. In 1965 a whole herd had crossed the valley for the last time; in the old days this was a regular occurrence. In the rainy season elephant from the Aberdare forests used to make their way to the Solai lake to take a cure in the salt grottoes; they then climbed up to the bamboo forests of Ol Joro Orok. Most of the tracks on the steep slopes of the Aberdares have been stamped out by elephant feet. These same slopes were home to rhinoceros and great herds of buffalo, but little by little the forests disappeared, giving way to farmland as Kenya's human population more than quadrupled.

Fortunately the birds did not desert us. So many and varied are they that it is impossible to identify them all just by colour or song. At Subukia I hear an emerald-green cuckoo saying "Hello Georgie" and another of the same species with a red crop that announces "It will rain"—and is very rarely wrong.

The last animal to depart is always the crafty leopard. His wants are few, or rather, he will eat anything. At night I hear leopard coughing as they roam around the farm. I always have to shut up my dogs at dusk, because they are no match for a leopard.

During my years in Africa I have been privileged to observe many kinds of wild animals but only when they allowed it, or when our paths crossed as we went our various ways. There are so many secret and inaccessible places in the Highlands, so many gullies and impenetrable forests in which unknown species of fauna may still be hidden, and some creatures long thought to be extinct may survive in the wild.

One of my friends, Josée Baradel, lived on the top of Ol Joro Orok at some 9,000 feet. She and her sister Mary were riding one day to Gilgil. They were descending a wide slope when they came upon a creature they had never seen before. It was hairy and looked like a small bear, young, clumsy and frightened. The two women were struck by its extraordinary rolling gait. When it moved it seemed as if it were mounted on ball-bearings. It had a short tail, and its back came up to about the bottom of Josée's stirrups. The two rode round it for a moment to take a closer look and then let it disappear. They never saw it again, and the encounter remained a mystery.

Mary told Louis Leakey, the paleontologist, about the strange sighting. He was extremely interested, and told her that he knew of a fossil creature with revolving joints, but it had been extinct for millions of years. However, Dr. Leakey admitted that it was not entirely impossible that in such remote and inaccessible areas some pairs of "living fossils" might survive. Two local tribes, the Kipsigis and the Nandi, are firm believers in the legend of the Nandi bear. According to them this is a bloodthirsty bear who stalks about at night and kills a great many cattle. This is, possibly, the African version of the Yeti, the Abominable Snowman.

I have heard it said by paleontologists that in prehistoric times different species of hominids at various stages of evolution might well have been alive at the same time, and even in the same places. I can just imagine an *Australopithecus* and a *Homo habilis* meeting in the bush and indulging in a bout of name-calling. But maybe I haven't understood properly. My friend Ismael, a Masai, is a firm believer in the folk tales he has heard in Narok. It seems that once upon a time some Masai warriors ran into a troop of men as hairy as baboons. In the ensuing fight a Masai threw a spear at one of the enemy and missed, and the hairy one picked up the spear and threw it back at its owner. Another legendary Kenya character was Ewart Grogan, a great traveller and businessman, and he relates in a book how once, in Uganda, he too saw a strange hairy being that was definitely not a gorilla. I do not know what credence should be given to these tales, but I know that they make capital subjects for conversation on long equatorial evenings.

With the approach of old age the Swifts retired on their 350-acre farm. They continued to watch over and help their African neighbours and could not envisage living anywhere other than Kenya, yet one day, in December 1992, Hobo was found unconscious on the floor of his studio in the middle of the afternoon with severe head wounds from an axe. He died a week later in hospital in Nairobi. He was loved, respected and admired by everyone, and no one could understand the reason for this terrible crime. The hunt for the murderer continues.

On Sundays, I often visit Billy Lambert. He is over eighty, a widower, and has trouble with his arteries, but he also has a great sense of humour. He lives in a big house, the home of the Governor at the time of the Mau Mau outbreak, Sir Philip Mitchell. Billy too has sold off his land but continues to help his neighbours by lending them his tractors. I enjoy visiting Billy as much for his wit as for the excellence of his table. He has an African cook renowned for such quintessentially English dishes as roast beef and Yorkshire pudding and lamb with mint sauce.

Billy's memories of his encounters with elephants are not happy ones. Some time in 1958 one of his farming friends came over to borrow a rifle in order to put a stop to the constant ravages of an elephant in his maize fields. In those days there was nothing shameful or illegal about shooting an elephant and Billy lent him a large-bore rifle and ammunition. Unfortunately, his friend used the wrong kind of cartridges, unsuitable for elephant and when the latter shot and wounded the creature, enraged, it charged him and stamped him to death. Billy got into hot water and was fined five hundred shillings. Although it was not illegal to kill an elephant, it was an offence to lend anyone a rifle.

Communicating with Africans can be a major problem in a country like Kenya, in which thirty-eight ethnic groups are recognized, each speaking their own tongue. Fortunately, there is a lingua franca—Swahili—which originated with the Arabs on the coast, who dominated commerce, and spread rapidly to become East Africa's common language. In Tanzania it is the official language; in Kenya it is on a par with English. Almost everyone in East Africa speaks at least two languages, that of their own tribal group and Swahili.

Swahili is a Bantu language enriched with Arabic. It is a beautiful and musical language and is easy to pronounce. Europeans are attracted by its fluidity and liveliness. Words like *jambo*, *karibu*, *hatari* and *pole-pole* are indelibly fixed in the memories of those who have made even a single voyage to East Africa. The snag comes when one tries to learn Swahili properly. It is by no means a primitive tongue: it is very elaborate, with an infernally difficult syntax. Even today, while I am able to communicate and make myself understood in Swahili, I am far from mastering its grammatical subtleties.

At Ol Kalou I had a teenage cook who had been to school and spoke English. He was not a very good cook, but he was useful as an interpreter with my staff. One day he asked me to double his wages.

"At Gilgil," he said, "there are officers who like their staff to speak English. If I go and work for them they will certainly increase my wages."

Unmoved by this naive blackmail, I gave him my blessing and told him to hurry off to Gilgil. Preferring to have a good cook rather than a good interpreter, I decided to apply myself seriously to the study of Swahili. Unfortunately, I did not go about it intelligently, by taking lessons with a teacher, and I got into bad syntactical habits, though later, in the seventies when AMREF organized courses for their European personnel, my Swahili did improve considerably.

Being able to speak the language properly changed my life, and clearly I should have tackled it seriously much sooner. Being able to communicate directly with many of my patients has facilitated my task as a flying doctor, and even in the most remote areas there is always someone, often an ex-soldier, who can translate the local tongue into Swahili.

Chapter 4

FLYING DOCTOR

I took my first flying lesson on 23 June 1963. I had always wanted to learn to fly, just as I enjoyed steering boats, riding horses and driving cars, and for the same reason: taming an animal or mastering an engine each brought a new kind of freedom. Until 1963 I had not had time or opportunity, but the changes that had disrupted Kenya and my own life made me decide that now was the time.

Kenyatta had just been elected prime minister and independence was imminent, with the obvious likely consequences, particularly an exodus of the European settlers who made up the core of my practice. I did not want to leave the country but the way forward was not clear. I was quite depressed, and taking to the air was both a means of escaping my problems and a great consolation. I had no idea that my new venture would lead to my joining Michael Wood and the flying doctors. All I did know in a confused sort of way was that I was at a crossroads, and had to find a new direction. Somewhere in my subconscious was the knowledge that learning to fly would be an asset in my future life.

My instructor, Bill Ford, was a superb pilot and a very unusual person. A South African, he had joined the South African Air Force in 1940. He was only sixteen and must have fudged his age to be accepted. After the war he joined the RAF in England as an instructor. He later served as a pilot in Kenya fighting the Mau Mau with the Rhodesian air force. He was demobilized in Kenya and became manager of a farm ten miles from Ol Kalou.

A number of us got together to form a flying group, a somewhat less formal arrangement than an aero club. We all pitched in to buy a little three-seater Piper, as well as guaranteeing its maintenance and insurance and our instructor's salary. Bill Ford happened to be free and took on the job. The club he had formerly worked for at Thomson's Falls had had to close down as the majority of its members were South African and had left the country.

The airstrip at Subukia was far from ideal for a trainee pilot. It is at the bottom of a narrow valley often visited by strong winds and turbulence and the surrounding mountain tops are often shrouded in cloud. The runway is a thousand yards long but take-off is only possible in one direction, to the north where the valley widens out. Also, at that altitude and temperature the air is thin, and in a small plane it can seem an age before the wheels leave the ground. Taking off was always more hair-raising than landing. If you muff an attempt at landing it is always possible to open up and go round again, but if you're unable to gain flying speed before the end of the strip—because the plane is too heavy, your speed is too low or there is a tail wind—then you are certain to end up in the bush. This can also happen when the grass on the strip is too long and slows acceleration.

Our Piper was not easy to pilot. It was a typical old tailwheeler, like all early planes. Taxiing such a plane is always difficult as it is very sensitive to crosswinds and can suddenly spin round 180°—known as "doing a rocking horse." If the pilot brakes too sharply or the ground is bumpy this tricky little plane is equally likely to do its "pylon" trick and end up with its prop in the grass and tail in the air.

Learning to fly these old machines is excellent training for pilots, because it teaches you delicate control and how to feel the plane making its way through often contrary air currents, calling for deft handling of the joystick and rudder bar. The modern tricycle undercarriage is very forgiving to the novice, and young pilots no longer seem to appreciate how their plane flies and or why sometimes they prang it.

Two or three times a week I used to fetch Bill at his farm and drive to Subukia. We always phoned the airfield first to ask how strong the winds were and whether the valley was clear of cloud. Sometimes the weather would deteriorate while we were en route and flying would be impossible by the time we arrived, but I was not about to let a little matter of a wasted sixty-mile round trip put me off.

I did not learn as fast as I had hoped. At forty-five, acquiring new reactions and reflexes is not as easy as when you are young. The thing I found hardest was judging height from the ground on landing so as to throttle back at the right moment. However, I soon learned to gauge my height by watching the grass at the edges of the runway. Everything, so far as planes are concerned, is a question of habit. When habit, through experience, becomes almost instinctive, one is nearly there.

I made my first solo flight in July 1963. All those who have learned to fly know that finding oneself alone in a plane is one of the most intensely moving experiences in life. After I had soloed, Bill Ford instructed me in navigating cross-country. A few minutes after take-off we flew over the immense pink splash of colour of Lake Nakuru with its thousands of flamingoes. Then we sighted the green-framed, dark-blue waters of Lake Naivasha, and the conical mouth of Longonot volcano. We returned via the foothills of Mount Kenya, with occasionally a glimpse of its snow-covered summit.

Flying over the Highlands and the Rift Valley was a continual enchantment and a wonderful reward for my long months of effort, doubt and, sometimes, fear. I had the feeling of being more closely bound to the country now that I could see it laid out below me from a pilot's privileged viewpoint.

In August I flew the mandatory triangular flight, between Subukia, Nanyuki and Nyeri in my case; flying a three-cornered course and touching down at two other airstrips without getting lost is a requirement for one's licence. It is the first non-local trip one takes without anyone to correct any navigational errors. This was one occasion on which I spent less time admiring the landscape than studying my map. Finally I went to Nairobi for the written examination—the papers on flight theory, air traffic regulations and so on. I found myself in a classroom with about thirty other candidates, among whom Mervin Cowie, a colonel in the Reserve and founder of Kenya's national parks, and I were the oldest, but it was we two "oldies" who passed, while the others failed one subject or another. Mervin Cowie was a remarkable man. He had led a very adventurous life, had known the writer Joseph Kessel and eventually joined AMREF as chief accountant. His 1952 book, *Where No Vultures Fly*, was made into an excellent film.

Like every newly qualified pilot, I wanted to fly as much as I could, or anyway as often as my heavy workload as a government doctor would allow. After years of being shaken to bits in a Land-Rover it was a relief and a real joy to sit comfortably at the controls of the capricious little Piper, even though it was so light that it could be severely buffeted by turbulence. I often flew to Nairobi and back and, as I had no radio on board, on arrival there I had to fly over the control tower and wait for an Aldis-lamp signal to land.

Bill Ford taught me prudence. Like all instructors he dinned the old adage, "There are old pilots and bold pilots, but no old, bold pilots" into his trainees. Kenya, and indeed the whole of Africa, is both beautiful and dangerous for pilots. There are no frosts or mists or overcast fronts as in Europe, but there are sudden storms and sometimes, near mountain slopes, downdraughts can slam you into the ground or up-draughts can whirl you up to an altitude where you are starved of oxygen. Even a blue sky can hold treacherous, invisible patches of turbulence. The magnificent landscape one longs to examine more closely is full of traps. There are volcano craters filled with lakes that can suck you down if you take too close a look—more than one plane has been found at the bottom of Longonot. One might fly low to view game and suddenly find an acacia tree filling the windscreen. Then there are hazards like the big marabou storks, which pay no attention to the rules of the air and can shatter a propeller or windscreen.

An incident at Subukia gave us all pause for thought. A few years earlier, Thomas, my original landlord at Subukia, had come to a tragic end. He had taken off for Nairobi with full tanks but had not taken into account the dense cloud cover. As he flew over the highlands he found himself jammed between two layers of cloud. Losing all idea of his position he began to fly round and round hoping to find a gap in the clouds. The control tower tried desperately to guide him to safety. "You have plenty of fuel, go east towards the coast, or west towards Lake Victoria, where you will be clear of cloud. Don't keep trying to get through where you are—you can't do it." But Thomas, determined to get through to Nairobi, obstinately refused to heed these warnings. After a while nothing more was heard from him. The police searched for him and when they gave up his wife paid a search party to hunt for a further week, but nothing was found. Ten years later the plane was found, empty and relatively undamaged, in a bamboo forest above Limuru with no sign of the pilot, whose fate remains a mystery to this day. As the Mau Mau were still operating in the district it was thought that they might have kidnapped him.

Today, I still use the same airstrip at Subukia. It is quite near my farm and I built a new hangar there. The land belongs to Africans who own a few strips of land in the vicinity, and each year I pay them a rent equivalent to what they would receive if they cultivated it. I am happy for them to graze their cattle on the airfield—an arrangement that suits us both as it keeps the grass down. They also keep an eye on potholes, and I ask them to make certain their animals are removed when I want to take off or land.

I bought my first plane in early 1964. It was a Piper Cherokee 235. At that time the American firm Piper were the market leaders in small single-engined planes with a new Cherokee series. In Nairobi they had an excellent agent, Wilken, whose office and repair shop at Wilson Airport was owned by John Williams and Michael Kennedy, and they made certain my plane was always kept in perfect order. I had chosen a very powerful machine equipped with a 235 horsepower engine. It could carry a cargo of 675 kilos—more than its own weight—which was quite exceptional, and it was the perfect machine to fly in Kenya, where one needs a plane that has both power and speed. Even on short high-altitude trips my Piper literally leapt into the air. Bill Ford helped me take delivery of it, and once again I was overcome with emotion at the thought of taking over the controls of a brand-new, powerful machine that had the added bonus of being all my own.

Michael Wood soon heard I had a new toy: "Anne, now that you have a lovely new plane and your licence, what are you waiting for to join us?"

At that time AMREF had only two planes, one belonging to Michael, which he flew himself, and another flown by a professional pilot, but more than two were needed for Michael's ambitious plans for his flying doctor service and he awaited my reply impatiently. I was, of course, tempted to join him at once, but I had first to work out my two-year contract with the District of Nyandarua.

In 1965 I made plans for my summer holiday. I intended going to Europe as usual, but this time I wanted to fly there in my own plane. I had no intention of impressing anyone by this, as many pilots had already done it before me, but it was a kind of personal challenge. In making this first big flight I wanted to prove myself as a pilot as well as my powers of endurance. I also wanted to increase my meager experience as a navigator and see regions of Africa as yet unknown to me. My friends, learning of my plans, were far from enthusiastic. "You're crazy," they cried. "Do you realize you are proposing to make a round trip of over seven thousand miles, flying over deserts and swamps in a single-engined plane?" They soon calmed down, knowing that I seldom went back on a decision. I merely wondered whether they would have had the same reaction if I had been a man.

Recently I was associated with an exhibition featuring women aviators staged in the Floral Park in Paris. I was extremely flattered at being thought to be in the same league as the famous airwomen whose feats were so much greater than mine. Closer acquaintance with the stories of their lives confirmed my suspicions that the combination of women and aeroplanes has long been thought of by the male sex as being "against nature." Yet, strange as it may seem, women took to the air very soon after men had made their first flights, not just as passengers but as pilots. It was only much later that men could bring themselves to admit this incredible audacity on the part of the weaker sex, and even today I wonder whether males will ever admit that women can be their equals as pilots. "Men don't believe in our potential," said the famous aviatrix Amelia Earhart. "They simply cannot believe that we can be any good."

Things were somewhat different in Kenya, where no one was too worried about what other countries did, and where women had often to fend for themselves, and we already had quite a number of excellent women pilots. For example, Beryl Markham became a world celebrity after accomplishing the first east–west flight across the North Atlantic, starting from England. Afterwards she returned to Kenya to continue her work as a racehorse trainer—and to provide regular news for the gossip columns.

I also knew June Sutherland, decorated by the Queen for her courageous exploits in the Congo war. In the thick of the fighting June landed on makeshift strips in order to evacuate to Rwandan women and children trapped in the Kivu. Thanks to her bravery many lives were saved. June had flown me on my first visit to Loyangalani and to Lake Turkana in 1961, a marvellous experience that I believe first inspired me to think seriously about becoming a pilot.

In the early summer of 1965 I had clocked up only 150 hours' flying time, but I was not as crazy as my friends imagined. I had no intention of undertaking the long and arduous flight to Europe solo, and had asked two good friends to accompany me. They were Dermott Bailey, a former navigator in the Royal Canadian Air Force who was to be in charge of the flight plans, weather forecasts and navigation, and his cousin, Tim Llewellyn, who would be baggage master—luggage had to be very carefully stowed in such a tiny plane and its proper placing was as complicated as a Chinese puzzle. Apart from piloting the plane, I had to act as flight engineer and also keep a close eye on the fuel.

Our first stopover was at Juba in southern Sudan. The town was crammed with refugees from the Belgian Congo—not then known as Zaire—which had been in the throes of civil war for several months. The Railway Hotel, the only one in town, had been invaded by refugees guarded by soldiers of the Sudanese army. We were lodged in pretty colonial-style pavilions with little cupolas behind the hotel, but food and drink were scarce.

The next day we undertook stage two of our flight with some trepidation, knowing we had to fly over the terrible marshes of the Nile, the Sudd, one of the most inhospitable areas in the world. From the air the land appears flat and green, but in reality it is a treacherous mixture of mud and water in which neither man nor beast—except crocodiles and mosquitoes—can move about or survive. God help anyone who comes down there, for the chances of rescue would be minimal, even if the plane were found. The four hours we spent flying over the Sudd seemed interminable, and the utter boredom of flying over a landscape through which we did not seem to be making any headway added to our anxiety.

I could not help remembering the sad misadventure that befell General Lewine and his wife some thirty years earlier. On his retirement the general had learned to fly and had become a proficient pilot, even winning the once-famous British King's Cup air race. He and his wife were flying to Kenya when engine trouble forced him to land his little plane in the middle of the swamps of the Sudd. The unfortunate couple had to spend eight days on a papyrus-covered island. They lived off the few provisions they had in the plane and drank water from the Nile. Fortunately, the surrounding water was not deep enough to harbour crocodiles, but they were attacked by hordes of mosquitoes, though with commendable forethought Mrs. Lewine had packed an umbrella and a mosquito net, which enabled them to rig up a makeshift shelter.

When they failed to arrive at their destination a search party was organized: a lost British general was top priority and the entire RAF was mobilized. Even the regular Imperial Airways passenger planes were asked to fly low and keep a sharp look-out for the Lewines. They were saved by the little mirror from Mrs. Lewine's dressing-case, which the general used to flash signals to passing aircraft. An RAF plane spotted them and threw them a survival kit, which unfortunately fell too far away for them to recover it. Eventually, there being no helicopters in those days, the stranded couple had to be rescued by the Sudanese by canoe. I knew General Lewine's widow, and she kept a little silver model of the plane that had nearly cost them their lives on a table at her farm at Njoro.

We were greatly relieved to touch down at Malakal, after which we once again picked up the Nile and followed it to Khartoum, where we planned to spend the night. Here I had my first brush with Sudanese officials since Port Sudan in 1948, the police were scandalized at my wearing slacks. I was furious.

"Do you expect me to pilot a plane in a skirt," I thundered. "I am the pilot and captain of this aircraft, do you understand?"

That a woman should be a pilot was bad enough but it was adding insult to injury to discover she was also a "captain"— their whole world seemed to be crumbling. They made me promise I would wear a dress in the hotel. I was ready to promise anything so long as they let me out of their furnace of an airport.

The following day we landed at Atbara. We had ordered fuel from Shell, which was delivered in twenty jerricans, each holding twenty litres. This meant a long and tiresome delay while we laboriously refuelled the plane. We then took off, leaving the Nile, which makes a big loop to the west. It was annoying to lose this easy navigational aid and fly over desert, in which good landmarks are few and far between. We had decided to follow the railway to Wadi Halfa on the Egyptian border; even though this meant a detour it was safer in case we needed to make a forced landing. There was a road running beside the railway track and at least one train a day, so we knew that if we broke down help would be available. We had to fly quite low to see the ground, as in summer the desert is very misty and we felt as though we were flying through a cloud of blue cotton wool.

The old town of Wadi Halfa was not yet submerged beneath the waters of the Aswan Dam and flying above Lake Nasser, which was beginning to take shape, we had some breathtaking views. The waters had not closed over the temples of Abu Simbel and we saw them in all their splendour just as they had originally been hewn into the cliff face.

As we neared Aswan on our way to Luxor, where we intended stopping off, the radio announced the imminent arrival of a fully fledged sandstorm, the terrible, hot, sand-laden desert wind that so often spoils visits to upper Egypt in summer. We had to put down at Aswan and wait for the storm to pass. When we finally arrived at Luxor we were forced into a lengthy wrangle with an airport health officer who refused to let us enter the town.

"You spent the night in Juba. They have meningitis there. You may well be contagious. No question of your leaving the airport."

We had been up since dawn, we were hungry and thirsty and it must have been at least 50°C in the shade. Finally, reluctantly, they let us go on condition that we went straight to a doctor to take massive doses of sulphonamides. We took a taxi downtown to a doctor, who made us swallow the tablets in front of him.

In spite of the intense heat we spent three days at Luxor in order to visit the temples and the Valley of the Kings. We then took off for Cairo, still flying in misty conditions. This time we reached a big airport in which we had to make full use of the radio. I had a few difficult moments trying to communicate with the air traffic controllers, as their English was not easy to understand, but they were extremely helpful in simplifying our approach.

After three days spent as eager tourists in Cairo, where we took in all the sights, from the museum to the Pyramids, we flew off again—to Crete. This was my first long flight over water. We were to fly nearly a thousand miles over the Mediterranean. Before leaving Nairobi I had taken the usual precautionary measures laid down in the aviation rule books by investing in—not stealing from an airline, as sometimes happens—an inflatable life raft and some Mae West life jackets from army surplus stocks. A long sea flight is always frightening, as one is only too conscious that for hours and hours there will be no reassuring landmarks to confirm one's navigation. At first I flew very high to save fuel, which is used up more rapidly at low altitudes, and also to maintain better radio communication in case of problems, but on nearing Crete I was obliged to fly almost at sea level since the cloud base was menacingly low and the weather atrocious. I had to circle for a good half-hour before landing at Heraklion in a violent storm.

After three days of touring Knossos and various antique sites—our trip had taken on a decidedly cultural aspect—we took off for Athens where we found ourselves in what amounted to an aerial traffic jam. Athens at that time was the stopover for commercial planes, whose range was far less than that of the aircraft of today, on their way to the Far East. I had to fight my way towards Athens guided by a crackling radio, through a multitude of Boeings coming and going. I felt lilliputian as the control tower talked me down to land on a taxiway between the two big runways reserved for jets—a wise precaution, because the eddies left by a big plane could overturn and flatten a Cherokee.

My family were awaiting me at Athens, and we went cruising in the Greek Islands. I didn't go near my plane for three weeks, and appreciated as never before the calm and silence, the stately progress and serenity of sailing. When the cruise was over we resumed our flight to Paris by way of Corfu, Rome and Cannes. Having proudly managed the first half of my epic journey I now began to regard myself as an experienced long-haul pilot. The second leg of the trip back was to make me eat a good helping of humble pie.

I wanted to end my holiday with my family in Alsace and Switzerland, which meant flying solo from Toussus-le-Noble airport to that of Basle–Mulhouse. The end of the summer was approaching, and the control tower weather forecasts were very pessimistic, as they so often are where private pilots are concerned, possibly to discourage them from being foolhardy. This does nothing to boost the confidence of a pilot preparing, perhaps a little nervously, for a long flight.

This was what happened to me. I took off too soon and immediately realized I would be completely lost in a fine and persistent drizzle. I no longer had Dermott on board to guide me, nor was my plane equipped with an automatic pilot. It is extremely difficult to pilot a plane and map read at the same time, so I pretended to have a minor technical fault and asked to return to Toussus. There I prepared a detailed flight plan, marking out all the alternative runways, radio beacons and roads, as I should have done from the start. Flying under visual flight rules (VFR) over France is not easy. The roads, railways, rivers and towns all look the same, so that eventually one becomes totally muddled and unsure where one has got to. That is why it is vital when flying to stick religiously to a meticulously prepared flight plan and follow its course exactly. This little misadventure taught me a salutary lesson.

From Mulhouse I hopped over to Zurich, where I left the Cherokee in the hands of the flight engineers to prepare for the flight home, and also met up with my flight crew, Tim and Dermott. After a stopover in Rome, we headed for Malta. Somewhere off Naples, Tim advised me that we had a fuel leak: a small but continuous stream of fuel was escaping under the right wing. I checked the fuel gauge and found it was dropping much too fast. I then checked the left-hand tank only to discover that the same thing was happening on that side, and all the while we were losing precious fuel.

We had just enough fuel to get us to Malta, where we spent several days trying to sort out the problem. A Maltese mechanic attached to the RAF came to help us but he could find nothing wrong so we decided to leave and fly straight to Libya and the Gulf of Syrta. About a third of the way there we discovered the leak had started again. Afraid that we might run out of fuel, we turned round and set course back to Malta, where we asked the tower to let us land immediately. They kept a BOAC jet waiting to enable us to do so.

This time we sent to Switzerland for a specialist from the Piper Company. He too was unable at first to find out what was wrong. Time was passing and we were becoming seriously worried. We all had work waiting for us in Kenya and it was obvious we couldn't stay forever in Malta. Fortunately for us, Dermott Bailey had relatives on the island and they kindly put us up at the Villa Rosa near Saint-George. Finally, the Swiss specialist discovered the reason for the leak: it was being caused by a joint at the fuel system drain cock. This is the lowest point of the system, through which the fuel is emptied during a service. At Zurich this joint had not been properly tightened, but the leak only occurred at a certain altitude when the atmospheric pressure lessened.

So much time lost, so much expense for a simple little rubber washer. I have noticed that mechanical faults discovered on planes are nearly always found after a service. The same often applies to cars, but usually with less serious consequences. Tim had to be back in Nairobi by a certain date, so he had to abandon us to fly back by commercial airline. Dermott and I found the return flight more demanding than the outward one had been. We were now flying against the prevailing winds with the sun full in our eyes, which did not help visibility. Furthermore, we were flying east, which lost us an hour's daylight each day. We were therefore obliged to take off at dawn so as not to lose precious time and be forced to lengthen our hops. This was not always easy: at Mersa Matruh on the Egyptian coast we had to take a taxi and go and winkle out the traffic controller to make certain he would be at his post at dawn so we could get away.

From Mersa Matruh we set course for Aswan, passing over the Qatar depression. We then flew straight to Khartoum, on our way passing through another sandstorm that forced us to fly at telegraph-pole level along the railway track, possible only because we knew there were no mountains or tunnels in the way. Time was of the essence and we pressed on, often in more than six-hundred-mile stages.

Between Khartoum and Juba we ran into a turbulent front. Some Air Sudan aircraft had turned back and for a moment we thought of doing the same, but Traffic Control encouraged us to press on. The atmospherics were violent but lasted only a short time, and we managed to get through with only a few jolts before landing and finding our way to the hotel, which was packed with refugees from the Congo.

The next day we got back to Kenya legally, in order to pass through Customs we should have flown straight to Nairobi, but I wanted to land at Subukia, where both Dermott and I were anxious to meet up with family and friends. In any case we had not brought back anything that could have been of the slightest interest to Kenya Customs. My finest trophy was my brand-new flight log with a respectable number of pages already filled. I have flown thousands of hours since, but have never made such a long flight.

It was without regret that in January I ended my work as a government medical officer in Nyandarua. It was getting more and more difficult to keep the service I had set up running properly. The County Council adminstration obstructed me at every turn, dragging his feet when it came to paying for anything. I had to finance the petrol for the fifty or more miles a day I was driving on official work. I had hoped to found a maternity hospital, but no funds were available for this project, and while my salary was a meagre thousand shillings a month, I was made aware that this was more than I was worth. Some of my colleagues had greater reserves of patience than I: Dr. Bunny at Naivasha, Dr. Lowy at Thomson's Falls and Dr. Rozinger at Malindi held out for a further two years before being obliged to quit their posts without even a thank-you for services rendered. The first push for the promotion of African doctors after Independence had begun, and European doctors had no option but to move out and make room for the newcomers. They were good, but they in their turn were no better treated than we were.

Having completed their medical studies, Kenyan doctors are obliged to work for five years in government service, although paid less than a fledgling typist. They have only one burning ambition, to be allowed to practise in a town in which they can earn a decent living, with no question at all of their going up-country where they are most needed. This meant the NGOs had to try to fill the gaps left by lack of government money and commitment. Michael Wood and the other founders of AMREF were well aware of this.

Michael Wood had arrived in Kenya in 1947 with his wife Susan and two young children. Why this young doctor, brought up in England in a family of civil servants, chose Africa is a matter of conjecture. He may have been influenced by the memory of the recent war and of the bombing. Or by the fact that he suffered from chronic asthma, which in his youth had forced him to spend five years in Switzerland; perhaps he hoped that the milder climate and high altitude of Kenya would improve his health. He came out for six months to help a surgeon in Nairobi who required an assistant. It did not take long for Michael and Susan to fall in love with Kenya, and soon after their arrival they decided to make it their permanent home. But they had reservations about living in town, with its endless round of cocktail parties and the like. They both felt that to get to know the Africans they must work closely with them, and the real core of African life is agriculture, so in 1950 the Woods bought a hundred and fifty acres of land at Limuru in the hills near the Aberdares, fifteen miles north of Nairobi.

"I knew absolutely nothing about farming," Michael admitted to me later, "but I learned from the earth. Here everything grows so quickly and one's efforts are soon rewarded if things go well; if they don't, you soon know it and simply start over again."

They built their first house themselves, and instead of the usual narrow Victorian-type windows so dear to the British, they broke with tradition by having big picture windows that framed to perfection the lovely views outside.

As Michael made closer contact with the Africans who lived and worked up-country he became aware of the appalling and needless injuries they suffered in what are called "domestic accidents." Their huts burned like torches, inflicting terrible burns on the occupants. Children were constantly at risk from unsupervised fires with cooking pots hanging over them. Toddlers falling into scalding water were an everyday occurrence. Farm labourers working with machines they did not understand constantly received serious injuries, and then there were injuries from wild animals or road accidents. All these mutilated and disfigured people so deeply distressed him that he went back to England to work under the famous plastic surgeon Sir Archibald McIndoe. He was convinced he would be of infinitely more use in Africa as a plastic rather than a general surgeon. On his return from England, Michael opened a consulting room in Nairobi, which was soon overflowing with patients. Sadly, however, he had begun his new career just at the moment when the Mau Mau were beginning their revolt, and every evening on his way back to their farm in Limuru, managed by Susan, he had to drive through the district that was the very nerve centre of Mau Mau activity.

On the farm, in spite of the wide cultural gap separating them, the Woods remained on very good terms with their employees.

"You are the tractor and we are the trailer," one of them remarked to Michael. Even so, everyone was aware that dramatic events were in the making—events that would mean tremendous changes for the white settlers.

"We didn't get much reliable information," Susan Wood said later, "but there were rumours and whisperings of strange and terrible ceremonies taking place in the forest, rites that then made no sense to us."

The gathering storm grew ever closer. Even at football matches there were no longer joyous shouts and cheers. Everything was conducted in total silence. Then came the State of Emergency. The Woods' farm was used as a centre for the police patrolling the district. Suspicion between the communities was rife and at nightfall people locked themselves into their houses. Many got rid of their firearms for fear of inviting attacks to steal them.

The Woods hung on grimly as long as they could, but eventually in 1957 they sold the farm in Limuru, which was not and had never been a profitable proposition, to a religious order. They bought a farm on the north-west slopes of Mount Kilimanjaro at Ol Molog. The property was in Tanganyika, which together with Uganda and Kenya made up what was then British East Africa. The new farm was larger than the previous one but it was also two hundred miles from Nairobi. Michael Wood obtained his pilot's licence and with two farmer friends invested in a Piper Tripacer. This allowed him to practise in Nairobi during the week and fly home to the farm at weekends. When I began work with him we both left Wilson Airport on Friday nights, each in our respective planes. He flew south while I flew north. Quite often we both called up the Foundation at the same time as we reached our homes:

"Foundation, Ol Molog in sight."

"Foundation, Subukia in sight."

Michael's former professor, Archibald McIndoe, also owned a farm in the area, where he spent his holidays. Another of his pupils, an American surgeon, Tom Rees, came to join them. The meeting of these three surgeons on the slopes of Kilimanjaro was to have far-reaching consequences, for it was during this encounter that the project which was later to become AMREF— the Flying Doctors of East Africa—was first mooted.

Archibald McIndoe was born in New Zealand. In 1931 he settled in England, and during the Second World War he became world-famous for his skills as a plastic surgeon, skills he used mainly in rebuilding the burned and shattered faces of the Allied pilots and aircrew wounded in the Battle of Britain. In his hospital at East Grinstead in Sussex he carried out three thousand five hundred operations in which he fashioned new noses and ears and remade burned faces using skin grafts. McIndoe had plumbed the depths of human pain and suffering. He was adored by the men to whom he gave hope and whom he restored to near-normal life. They banded together and proudly called themselves the "Guinea-Pig Club."

Tom Rees came from a Mormon family in Salt Lake City, where his father was a professor of biology. Sent to Nairobi on a surgical mission, Tom was shocked by the terrible injuries of some of the patients he saw there. Fresh from a world of sanitized American hospitals, he was devastated by the pain suffered by children with horrific burns, and by eyelids deformed by trachoma or leprosy. Without eyelids, a patient cannot sleep and is threatened by both exhaustion and blindness.

McIndoe and Rees had fallen under the spell of Africa with its magnificent landscapes and wildlife, the buffalo, gazelle and giraffe over which Michael Wood would fly low when showing his colleagues the splendours of his adopted country. The three men found it difficult to relate to so much human misery amid such natural beauty, and they also knew that the African patients they saw in the hospitals in Nairobi represented only a fraction of the sick and injured out in remote places or deep in the bush. They spent hours discussing the situation. Eventually they came to the conclusion that the only possible solution was to change the existing order: instead of hoping that the sick would find their way to Nairobi, medical help should be made available to them where they lived. This revolutionary thinking was later endorsed by the Declaration of Alma-Ata in 1977, when at a conference in Kazakhstan, the World Health Organization announced that medicine should go to the patient and not the other way round. McIndoe liked to repeat the following saying: "All surgeons should spend some time with primitive peoples, in so doing doctors would acquire further skills, and man would find his soul."

It was decided to set up an organization to provide mobile medical assistance to remote mission settlements but also to undertake research. This region of Africa is of unique interest, in being divided into separate ethnic groups that occupy separate regions and that do not mix with one another. This situation points up some interesting medical enigmas. For example, the Masai, who drink only the milk and blood of their cattle, have a pre-eminently high-cholesterol diet, do not suffer from coronary heart disease. On one side of a mountain one can find a tribe subject to localized cancers, on the other a population that is immune, or suffers from different kinds of cancer.

By common consent the new organization was given the name African Medical and Research Foundation, after which, like the Apostles, the three surgeons went their different ways to spread the word and raise money for the new foundation. McIndoe went to England, Tom Rees back to the United States, leaving Michael Wood alone to face up to Africa's problems.

Although he was an experienced pilot and had on occasion used his plane to visit distant patients, Michael Wood did not at first think in terms of using aircraft. There were flying doctors in Australia, but that was already a highly developed country in which flying was an accepted mode of transport, airstrips were common and the standard of living was high enough to enable Australians to buy and maintain their own planes. There was nothing comparable in East Africa.

With the first funds raised for the young foundation Michael bought lorries and had them equipped with an operating theatre, a dispensary and a radio. He had set himself a formidable task at a time when the whole world was more concerned with liquidating the colonial empires than with providing medical aid to the Third World, but he brought to it immense strength of character allied to great charisma. He was tall and slightly stooped owing to his asthma. He had a mass of blond hair, which as the years advanced turned to silver, and deep blue eyes whose level gaze reflected something of the energy and vitality that drove him. He brought intense concentration to everything he did, whether operating, flying or simply conversing with someone. His charm and powers of persuasion were precious assets in his indefatigable pursuit of funds for AMREF.

Susan, Michael's wife, was also a very special person. She too was possessed of great inner reserves of strength. Apart from her role as wife and mother of four children, two boys and two girls, she found the time and the talent to build and decorate her homes; when fire gutted the house at Ol Molog it had to be rebuilt from scratch. Susan met Michael when she was a nurse and he, after flirting with the idea of becoming an architect, was completing his medical studies. The war had taken its toll on these two young people. Susan's father and uncle died in the rubble of a bombed building in London and her brother Lionel was killed at Salerno, while Michael's elder brother was lost at sea in a Royal Navy destroyer.

Africa was in Susan's genes: she was born in the Congo in a mud hut decorated with tea chests and mosquito-netting.

"My birth was an event," she once told me, "and news of my arrival was spread through the forest on African drums. I was the first white baby to be born in the depths of the Congo bush."

Her father, born in Japan, had decided to become a doctor, but at twenty-one had abandoned medicine to become a missionary. When Susan was a year old, her parents strapped her into a hammock and she travelled with them on the long journey on foot from the Congo mission station to the Nile. They embarked at Juba, in southern Sudan and sailed down the Nile to Alexandria, where they boarded a steamer bound for England. The journey took six months, and tested the character and powers of endurance of the little girl.

After this heroic journey Susan's father decided to return alone to Africa, rejoining his family every three years. He went to northern Kenya to evangelize the El Molo and Turkana people and then travelled to Ethiopia. Erudite and an excellent linguist, he translated the Coptic Bible from the original text into modern Amharic, and presented the finished work to Emperor Haile Selassie. His prolific life was ended in 1940 by the same bomb that killed his brother as the two dined together in London.

In 1963, when I first got to know of the work being done by AMREF, the lorries of the mobile unit were proving something of a disappointment, as they were quite unequal to the workload Michael expected of them. They were cumbersome vehicles that often got bogged down or broke down in the rainy season.

Michael soon realized that a mobile operating theatre in a lorry
was not practical, and that far better results could be obtained
by liaising with existing hospitals run by missions or by government. By giving them up-to-date equipment and visiting them
simply to operate, both time and money would be saved. But
another plane would be needed.

Some years earlier Arthur Godfrey, a famous American TV
presenter, had given AMREF a twin-engined Piper Aztec, which
by this point had reached the end of its useful life. To refit it
would have cost a fortune. Luckily, Godfrey then presented
AMREF with a second plane, a Cherokee 235, which was far
more economical to run than the twin. The following year,
Misereor, a Catholic organization, gave AMREF a Cessna 206
Skywagon, and Michael Wood swapped his worn-out Cherokee
180 for a twin-engined Comanche. Finally, in April 1967, the
efforts of Leonora Semler bore fruit. Leonora, wife of a German
politician, had been one of the first people to embrace our cause
and she moved heaven and earth in Germany to attain her ends.
Thanks to her efforts the Bonn Government sent us a munificent
gift in the shape of another Cessna 206, together with a financial
grant to cover its operating costs for two years.

Leonora Semler had also managed to obtain twenty-five radio
transceivers for AMREF, which brought the number of our radio
stations in outlying hospitals and missions to seventy-three. At
long last the flying doctors had the means to carry out their
plans.

AMREF's finances were handled by Bill Bunford who, on retir-
ing from Shell, had become our financial director. He introduced some tough financial cuts in our budget. Finance was not
one of Michael's strong points, but Bunford knew what he was
doing, and saw to it that the Aztec was sold and that we moved
out of our expensive office premises in the middle of Nairobi to
cheaper prefab shacks at Wilson Airport.

At that time there were only two flying doctors, Michael and
myself. I had been taken on as a replacement for Roy Schaeffer,
who wanted to return to the States to supervise his children's
education. He was a very experienced doctor and had already

taken part in the mobile unit adventure. I was far from being an experienced flying doctor but I was no debutante either. The previous year, while I was still working for the government at Ol Kalou, Michael had asked me to undertake a number of medical missions in Turkana whenever I had a break or a holiday.

The plan was to give support to Dick Anderson, the missionary doctor at Lokori Hospital, south-west of Lake Turkana. Anderson was convinced that a team of flying doctors would be of immense benefit to his patients, and so anxious was he to bring this about that he had a number of landing strips built in his area to await the glorious day when the first flying doctor should land at Lomelo. I was to be the first to have this privilege. In my log book I made notes of the landings in red ink. I was quite proud of these particular exploits, as the landing strips were far from easy to approach, and at that time I had only clocked up about sixty hours of flying time. Dick Anderson was the only doctor in the whole of Turkana, a vast semi-arid district measuring some sixty by a hundred and twenty-five miles. Not only was he in charge of Lokori Hospital and that of Kakuma, run by a Catholic mission, but he was also responsible for the Lokitanng and Lodwar government hospitals. It was the first year of Independence, and government doctors were still few and far between. Our job as flying doctors was to service the various hospitals in this network. Having examined the patients on the spot, we ended our rounds by taking those in need of intensive treatment to Lodwar. It was here that Dr. Anderson, who was also a surgeon, operated. Sometimes, when plastic surgery was necessary, he would be joined by Michael Wood.

On the principle that people only appreciate what they have to pay for, Dr. Anderson charged his patients a purely symbolic fee of one or two shillings, or one of the ornaments they wear. The Turkana place leaves of aluminium in their noses or ears, or they insert a spent cartridge case or a bone or ivory tube in their lower lip. The tube is then filled with tobacco which they can sniff all day long.

One of their customs, the ritual extraction of two incisor teeth from the lower jaw, was useful from a therapeutic point of view. In tetanus, which was common, the jaw muscles go into spasm and the patient cannot open his mouth, but it was possible to insert a tube or straw through this gap in the teeth to enable a patient to be rehydrated and fed.

Besides the strips Anderson had constructed near the hospitals, he had others built close to some of the small villages. The second time I touched down at Lomelo we found ourselves in the midst of a local fiesta. Dressed in ceremonial robes, and bristling with ostrich feathers, the Turkana looked magnificent. In spite of the festivities we carried on with our clinic as usual. We were about to leave and were having a cool drink in a *duka* when we heard loud screams. A man came hurtling through the door of the store and threw himself at our feet, begging us to protect him. He was already pretty battered and was covered with blood. We calmed him down, and bit by bit he told us what had happened to him. He was a Masai from Mount Elgon who had had the foolish idea of making advances to a Turkana woman. This had annoyed the Turkana men, who wanted to kill him, and were waiting outside the store to finish off the job. We wondered what on earth he was doing so far from his own part of the world. We cleaned him up, bandaged him and gave him some medication, but there was no question of our taking him back with us—the plane was already full. We hustled him out of the shop through the back door. He was off like an arrow, with his assailants close on his heels. I hoped they would not catch up with him for I knew he would not escape from them alive.

It was only recently that I heard the end of this story. Our Masai swain survived. He managed to get to Lokori where the missionaries took him in. He was certainly quite an athlete.

At one end of the runway at Lokichar was a heap of big boulders, at the other end some very tall trees. In spite of these obstructions I was fond of the place. We used to hold our clinics in the middle of a clearing in a grove of giant acacia trees close to the corrugated iron house of the local schoolmaster. While Anderson was treating his patients, I used to go and sit on a big stone that intrigued me. It looked like a gravestone and you could see chisel marks on it. I asked for it to be turned over, and found, as I had suspected, that it was a tombstone with an inscription in English. It was a tribute to the courageous exploits of a Sudanese sergeant-major who had served in the police. He had died some twenty-five miles away near the river. He must have been greatly respected by his superior officers, for they had clubbed together to pay for his tombstone. We deduced that the lorry carrying the stone to the grave must have broken down at Lokichar, and that the stone had been abandoned here. The dead soldier and his epitaph were never united.

Dick Anderson was with me when I had my first accident. This took place on the runway of Lobokat, a village in the middle of the bush. The strip was short and narrow, and to add to my difficulties, dust-devils whirled around us, making it almost impossible to determine wind direction. I was holding the nose of the plane as high in the air as possible, intending to make a short landing. I was about ten feet off the ground when the plane stalled suddenly, and we landed with a severe bump. One wheel broke off, the undercarriage dug into the ground on that side, and we came to a halt within ten yards, after a magnificent "rocking horse" turn.

So there we were, stranded and crippled, hidden away in a place so remote that it was known only to Anderson, myself and Michael Wood, who had already touched down there. We realized that if we were unable to contact him we were in for a very long wait so we flung ourselves at the radio, pulling out the aerial—at that time a long wire wound on a reel that had to be unwound to make a call.

By pure good luck Michael was at the Foundation, and was able to give precise instructions as to our location to my old friend Bill Ford, who was still our chief pilot and within four hours a rescue plane carrying a mechanic and spare parts had arrived. Meanwhile we had held our clinic and asked some men to help us lengthen the airstrip. This was vitally important as my damaged aircraft was taking up half the strip, and was stuck in such an awkward position that it was impossible to dislodge her.

Bill Ford managed to land without incident, but when the mechanic was getting his tools together, I heard him shout: "I've forgotten one of the most important parts of the lot—the axle for the wheel. I'll have to go back to Nairobi to fetch it."

He would never make the journey there and back before nightfall, so the repairs would have to wait until the following day. We waved him goodbye, and went off to spend the night at the hospital at Lokori, quite close to Dick Anderson's house.

I had a few other bad moments at Lokori. On one occasion I simply could not land. I tried once, twice, three times, but I was going too fast and I knew there was a deep gully at the end of the runway. I went round quite a few times before I realized that the wind had changed direction, which was a very rare occurrence. There was no wind sock nor any smoke to guide me down, as nobody had thought to light a fire. It may be that the missionaries always rely on the Lord to provide divine intervention at crucial moments and think pilots do not need any other kind of help. Smoke is still the best way of gauging wind direction. We had asked for a windsock to be installed but the Turkana regard a windsock as a most useful item and invariably steal it. At Lodwar, the main town in the district, the windsock is in the prison courtyard out of their reach.

At one clinic we asked for a windsock and provided detailed, clear instructions on how to make one. On our next visit there it was attached to its mast but hanging limply downwards in spite of a stiff breeze. They had taken the "sock" part too literally and sewn up the toe—the idea of a sock that was open at both ends had seemed silly.

Dick Anderson was also a minister and he used to hold his services and preach in Turkana, which he spoke fluently. He and his wife were both very musical and they taught their congregation to sing strange but astonishingly beautiful tunes.

"They are traditional Turkana airs," Dick explained, "adapted to the psalms translated into Turkana."

We had brought a projector with us to Lodwar to show the nomadic shepherds an educational film on modern veterinary methods. The film showed close-ups of animals being vaccinated.

The whole village, resplendent in the plumes and necklaces, had turned out to watch the film. When the film ended the entire audience broke into a harmonious chant, which came to an abrupt halt. The interpreter explained the meaning of the chant:

"They have just told you they are not interested in what you have shown them. They would not be able to use your methods on their animals."

Without any visible signs of consultation the nomads had expressed their opinion of vaccination in a grave and melodious incantation. Their singing reminded me of a Gregorian chant with words from the Gospel but in fact the words were improvised on the spot. We were amazed and hurriedly packed up our equipment to some embarrassment. To this day I have not fathomed the secret of the instant protest songs of the Turkana.

We were always made welcome by the various tribes, even those who had never seen an aeroplane. So far as rural Africans are concerned white people are capable of anything, so nothing they do surprises them.

At Lobokat Dick Anderson and I once had an uncomfortable experience. A youth had been brought to us suffering from gangrene of the jaw, probably the result of a clumsy dental extraction. The boy was in a bad way, suffering from shock and with a very high temperature. He urgently needed penicillin and surgery, so we decided to fly him back to the hospital at Lokori. We had got him into the plane when a hideous, toothless, white-haired old woman arrived, shouting and gesticulating. She looked like a witch—which indeed she was. Dick Anderson translated:

"She does not want you to take the boy away. He has to stay here and she will look after him."

I didn't agree, but she was backed up by a group of Turkana warriors, who were closing round us brandishing their spears. Dick and I were alone so further argument would have been unwise, since the men were clearly much in awe of the old witch and would not have hesitated to spear us. We unloaded the poor boy and handed him over to her. I very much doubt he survived.

A major problem in Turkana is hydatid disease, caused by a

small tapeworm, carried by dogs, whose eggs are broadcast in dog feces. The ova get onto grass and plants and are then eaten by herbivores or, by mischance, by humans. The larvae hatch and make their way usually to the liver, lungs or the intestinal mesentery, where they grow into enormous fluid-containing cysts that can weigh several kilos. These contain thousands of embryo tapeworms, and the natural cycle is for the herbivore to die and a dog to be infected by eating its flesh. The Turkana have the highest rate of human infection in the world, which is not surprising considering in what short supply water for washing is in a desert climate. Affected patients develop enormously swollen bellies. I remember seeing a photograph in a travel magazine of myself examining a young Turkana woman with a very distended abdomen. The caption said I was conducting an antenatal examination, though in fact the poor woman was suffering from a large hydatid cyst. The mistake is understandable because the disease is little known in the West, though it crops up from time to time in Muslim communities when uninspected meat is eaten after illegal slaughtering; the Echinococcus tapeworm is no stranger in Marseilles hospitals.

For a long while the only treatment was to remove the cysts by surgery, but there is always a danger of recurrence—only one tapeworm embryo needs to escape into the abdomen during the operation for the whole process to begin over again. Today, we use chemotherapy with albendazole as well as surgery, but it is a toxic drug and only successful in about fifty percent of cases. The best remedy against this scourge is prevention, but unfortunately it is almost impossible to change traditional customs. When a Turkana warrior finds a cyst in the liver of a goat he has just killed, he cuts it out and throws it on the ground where it is snapped up by dogs. The dog's feces infect the grass and this is eaten by camels, sheep or goats who thus play their part in the tapeworm life cycle. Worse still, like the Masai, the Turkana do not bury their dead but leave them out to be devoured by wild animals, so if they are infected, the infection is passed on to the jackals or other scavengers.

This vicious circle is difficult to break. The domestic dog is the weakest link in the chain and we had our greatest success when we persuaded the nomadic tribes to put down their stray dogs and retain only their trained sheepdogs. These are given powerful deworming pills and their feces are burned. Although most hydatid cysts develop in the lungs or abdomen, they can lodge anywhere—I once saw one that was growing in the eye-socket and was pushing the eyeball outwards.

In the course of 1964 our team was joined by a flying nun; a twenty-year-old American Catholic nurse called Sister Michael Therese. Her father was serving in the U.S. Air Force in Germany and she had learned to fly a plane on the military base to which he was attached. She had come to Kenya to work with the Medical Mission of Mary run by Irish missionaries. The good fathers had been given a little plane, a Cessna 182, for which they had not much use, since none of them could fly it and in any case there was no spare cash to maintain it. They were therefore only too delighted to come to an arrangement with Michael Wood whereby AMREF would be responsible for the maintenance and running of their plane. This arrangement was to remain in force until the purchase price of the little Cessna was reached, when the plane would become the property of the flying doctors. It was a typical African trade.

The obvious choice for pilot was Sister Michael Therese. She managed very well and was able to land wherever her services were needed. She was a good pilot but knew very little about the mechanics of her plane. One day I met her looking worried. "I've been flying this plane for six months," she said, "and I'm beginning to wonder whether I should not top up the battery. Do you know where it is?"

I said I had a vague idea. I lifted the engine cowling and showed her a little box. "I think it's in there."

"Son of a gun!" she exclaimed. "Who would have thought it!" Son of a gun was her favourite expletive, and suitably innocuous for a nun.

Sister Michael Therese must have had a vigilant guardian angel. Once in Uganda her plane developed a serious oil leak just as she was flying over Amudat, a Protestant mission. She spiralled down and landed without damage on a big square piece of land. She wanted to take off again at once and was not inclined to obey the instructions she was given through the radio.

"Tell me what to do to repair the leak but don't make it too complicated. I want to get out of here now."

"No, no," pleaded Michael Wood, anxious for her safety. "Just sit tight. We'll come and fetch you. Just be patient; don't push your luck."

Sister Michael Therese took on the AMREF circuit in Turkana. She was based at the hospital at Lodwar, where she was joined by a nun who was a surgeon. This meant that this area was well provided with medical aid, particularly as Dr. Anderson was beginning to receive help from an American Protestant organization, the Missionary Aviation Fellowship. We had started the ball rolling and could now direct our efforts to other areas badly in need of our help.

In 1965 Turkana was in the grip of a severe famine. Since I knew the area pretty well I was asked to undertake a tour to evaluate the effects on the local populations. We were to co-operate on this project with Brother Mike, an American Marist brother who taught at Nairobi's Mangu High School. He also worked for Wings for Progress an association, funded by the U.S. government, whose purpose was to transport missionaries, no matter where or when, all over Kenya. I wondered whether perhaps the CIA, was not helping to subsidize this project, for these missionary flights were an ideal cover to observe all that was happening in the various countries they visited. Brother Mike's assistant and co-pilot was nicknamed Brother George despite the fact that he was not a missionary. He was a decent chap, but, I was to find out, rather reckless. He was chosen to fly our team to Turkana. When he came to pick me up at Nakuru in the Cessna 206 he already had two other passengers aboard—Mr. Foot sent by the government and an Irish nursing sister. Then we flew to Kitale where George took on two other passengers, and at the last minute picked up an unscheduled passenger, a Catholic nun who wanted a lift home to Kakuma.

This made seven of us on board together with our luggage and equipment. The runway at Kitale is very long but is at an altitude of 6,500 feet, and the grass was quite high. I was beginning to wonder how on earth we were going to manage to take off. I was only the co-pilot and had no idea what the plane was capable of, so I kept quiet. George opened the throttle and we began to gather speed. The plane left the ground and then came down again. The end of the runway was near, and we were still not airborne. The nun from Kakuma was terrified and wanted to get out.

"Stop, George, please, let me get off."

George braked and made a half-turn. He was perfectly calm. "I know exactly what happened," he said, "I'll make a fresh start." He then explained to me that he had not managed to get the fuel mixture right for that altitude, but that from now on all would go without a hitch. His passengers did not share his optimism. There was panic both inside and outside the plane. People were rushing about waving their arms, and a jeep was hurrying towards us. Everyone was shouting at George to let the passengers out. The nun from Kakuma was beside herself. George was adamant.

"I know what I'm doing. This time there won't be any trouble."

So off we went. The Cessna became airborne only at the very last moment. As we climbed, nose up, the stall warning sounded continuously until we reached the edge of the plateau and could put our nose down. Being a pilot at such moments has its disadvantages, since I knew exactly what was happening.

We were on our way to Lokori where we had to put off two passengers. In winning tones George said, "I'm counting on you, Anne dear, to guide me down as I don't know this place at all."

That was all we needed, and my heart plummeted into my boots. The runway at Lokori is very narrow, with rocks and a deep ravine at one end. You have to land very short and brake at once. I simply could not imagine how a pilot who did not know the strip could possibly land such a heavily laden plane successfully. Rather than irritate George, I hatched a little plan: I guided him to Kangetet, an old wartime airfield three miles from Lokori with a very wide runway that was certainly a much safer bet than Lokori's airstrip. George circled the area, lost sight of the runway and came down too low, but at the third attempt managed to land without incident. He was a bad pilot. He then taxied as far as some *dukas* near the airfield, where he was told that he was not at Lokori but at Kangetet. He was furious, but so was I.

"You would never have managed to get us down safely at Lokori. You barely made it here, which is child's play. Use the radio to call the hospital. They will come and fetch you, or if you don't want to do that you can walk the three miles to Lokori."

Finally, Brother George did fly the team all over Turkana, but I would only go with him under certain conditions and I kept a sharp eye on his handling of the plane. At the end of the trip, when he dropped me off at Nakuru, George confessed that the engine of the Cessna was at its last gasp and had few hours of life left in it. This, of course, accounted for the lack of power. What troubled me was the fact that although George knew he had a clapped-out old plane, he insisted on doing the flight and endangering all our lives. I came to the conclusion that although he was not a priest he had spent so much time with the good fathers that he felt, like them, that he was under God's special protection.

As soon as I became a permanent member of AMREF I was given the task of inaugurating flights to north-east Kenya—to Marsabit district. I made a first recce of the strips with Bill Ford, taking in Loyangalani, North Horr, Ileret and the police station at Sabarei. Later we added Dukana, Sololo and Moyale to the list. I still follow the same itinerary today, but at that time conditions were very different. We were engaged in bitter conflict with Somalia, which laid claim to North Kenya and maintained armed marauding bands. Villages were constantly attacked and looted, their cattle stolen. Before landing up there I had to wait for an army Land-Rover carrying a machine-gun to come and guard the airstrip. The only way to travel by road was to go in convoy, with a military escort trained to detect landmines.

The Somalis are enterprising shopkeepers. Trading is in their blood, and they will set up shop in even the tiniest of hamlets. Their *dukas* are always surrounded by relatives in their tribe. Their relative wealth compared with that of the nomads gives them a certain political clout. They think of themselves as Somalis rather than Kenyans, a point those in power in Mogadishu repeatedly make.

The local population suffered greatly at the hands of these warring factions, and their distress was aggravated when, in 1966, the ravages caused by the bandits were followed by a two-year drought and a famine.

I was resting at Subukia one day when I was telephoned from the Foundation: "Anne, you are needed at Moyale to pick up a woman who has been seriously wounded and evacuate her to Nakuru."

The last part was no problem, as Nakuru is near my home, but Moyale, on the Ethiopian border, is all of two hundred and fifty miles to the north. The journey there and back would take most of the day. I asked for details of the patient's injuries and was told she had been badly hurt in an attack in which her whole family had been massacred. She was the sole survivor. The *shiftas* had attacked in the dead of night, and she had hidden under her bed. These beds are wooden frames fixed on posts set in the ground and are covered by a large animal-skin rug that conceals the narrow space under the pallet, into which a very slim person can just squeeze.

One of the *shiftas* stuck his spear through the bed to make certain there was nobody hiding beneath. The spear pierced her stomach, but she managed not to cry out and give herself away. She stayed there for the rest of the night, not daring to move. At dawn, friends from a neighbouring village found the hapless woman and took her to the hospital at Moyale, where she was given antibiotics and sedated. The hospital then called AMREF to get her transferred to a larger hospital. The weather was poor, and I had to circle above the airfield for some time before the police arrived. The strip right next to the hospital was unusable, so I had to land on another one some distance away. While waiting for my patient, I refuelled from jerricans I had brought with me. Weather reports made me suspect that I might have to make a detour on the return journey.

On leaving I had to climb to about 10,000 feet to get above the cloud covering the Matthews Range, but the radio informed me that Nakuru was in the clear and I could carry on. It was at this precise moment that the patient woke up. Imagine the reactions of a good lady, who had never seen anyone but her family and friends, their camels and the bush, on suddenly finding herself 10,000 feet up in the air in a tiny cabin.

Panic-stricken, she began to yell at the top of her voice. She then undid her seat belt and tried to throw herself out of the door. I had to keep the plane steady with one hand, while, with the other, trying to keep her in her seat. I tried to reason with her but she did not speak Swahili. Finally I offered her something to eat—I think it was a biscuit—and this seemed to pacify her. Having regained confidence in her novel mode of travel she promptly fell asleep. Had the patient been a robust male instead of a slight female, things might have turned out differently, and there and then I swore never again to travel alone with a patient.

The ambulance was waiting at Nakuru airfield and the surgeons were standing by at the hospital. It was 6 p.m. and there was just enough daylight left for me to get back to Subukia.

Three months later I passed through Nakuru. At the hospital a woman called out to me. It was my patient, now fully recovered. She had acquired a little Swahili, sufficient for us to carry on a conversation. I said:

"You are much better. Next month I shall be coming to take you home."

She smiled, a very sweet smile. This time she had no qualms about flying.

In those days Africa was in turmoil. All the neighbouring countries around were experiencing the turbulence that goes with obtaining independence, and compared with them Kenya was an island of peace and stability, apart from its trouble with Somalia. In 1964 the Sultan from the Omani family that had ruled Zanzibar for centuries was deposed in a bloody revolution and Zanzibar and Tanganyika united to form Tanzania.

In that same year Rwanda and Burundi, once governed by Belgium, became independent and split into two separate and hostile countries. This created one of the most potentially explosive and dangerous situations in the whole of Africa. In Rwanda, as in Burundi, the minority Tutsi refused to admit the claims of the majority Hutu. As an added complication, the two warring communities came from totally different peoples: the Hutus are Bantu, while the Tutsi are Nilo-hamitic. One did not have to be a prophet to predict the vicious internecine strife that resulted, with appalling massacres and massive population displacement. Refugees in their hundreds of thousands sought sanctuary in neighbouring countries, including Tanzania, which had to hastily improvise camps for the footsore and exhausted refugees. For a time I visited one of these camps, Mwesi in south-west Tanzania, near Lake Tanganyika, every two months. It was a long 600-mile, five-hour flight, including a refuelling stop at Tabora en route.

Mwesi is situated high up on the slopes of a mountain, and consequently the weather there is often bad. More than once I have had to return to Tabora after being unable to land at Mwesi. For much of the year the place is enveloped in a dense fog that blots out the lake, twenty-five miles away. When the weather is fine and clear, the Mahari mountains rising from the immense stretches of the lake are a magnificent sight. The Mahari mountains are also known as the "Mountains of the Moon," a common name in Africa as *mwesi* is Swahili for moon.

The refugee camp was run by Swedes from the Tanganyika

Christian Refugee Service, a Lutheran organization. The Swedish doctor in charge had two nurses to assist him, one German, the other Dutch. My main role was to act as courier, bringing vaccines and medicines. Tanzania is a very large country, twice the size of Kenya, though with the same population, and the capital, Dar es Salaam, is six hundred miles from Mwesi. At that time it lacked any infrastructure, especially in the west of the country.

At Mwesi camp I again had the privilege of watching that exceptional plastic surgeon Michael Wood at work. The nurses brought him a ten-year-old boy with a hideously disfiguring harelip. Since our time at Mwesi was limited, Michael decided to operate the day after we arrived, although, not expecting to operate there, he had not brought his surgical instruments. The hospital was poorly equipped, but Michael swept away all obstacles, declaring cheerfully that all he needed was a good pair of scissors, a scalpel, a forceps and a needle and thread. The operation took place on an ordinary kitchen table. The patient did not seem in the least alarmed. Wood chatted to him, explaining that he would be given an injection and would feel no pain. Meanwhile, he was using a ballpoint to sketch the outline of his incision on the patient's face. He explained what he was doing to the doctor and nurses round the operating table.

"I need to draw my guide lines before the local anesthetic takes effect, as it will make the tissues swell and everything will be distorted."

The boy was given an intravenous injection of pethidine to sedate him, after which the local anesthetic was injected and Michael went to work. After a few swift, deft incisions and some stitches, the fifteen-minute operation was over. Michael patted the boy's shoulder and carried him back to bed. By the next day the swelling had gone down and the spectacular result of the operation was visible. Michael Wood had once again proved himself a magician who could successfully carry out the most intricate operation with very few instruments at his disposal.

Seeing the hundreds of completely destitute refugees was heart-breaking. They had lost everything when they fled, and no end to their misfortunes was in sight. Thirty years later peace still has not returned to Rwanda and Burundi, which, with their fertile hills and pleasant, healthy climate, could be a kind of African Switzerland were it not for the never-ending wars and the population explosion. The majority of the population is Christian, predominantly Catholic, so birth control, of course, is not acceptable. Furthermore, the incidence of AIDS is among the highest in the world.

This was my first encounter with refugees from mass murder and genocide in Africa; like a plague, it no sooner is contained here than it breaks out there. Since then I have seen streams of refugees arriving in Kenya—Ugandans, Ethiopians, Sudanese, Somalis. Today they still come in their hundreds. I shall never be sufficiently hardened to this scourge.

I ran into quite a number of problems on my long flights to and from Mwesi. A sudden encounter with vultures cost me a buckled silencer and an open oil cover. Another incident could have had far more serious consequences. Somehow I had let myself get trapped in a bank of clouds. I could see nothing but white all around. This is a classic, and often fatal, trap for pilots who have not trained in flying blind on instruments. One very quickly becomes completely disoriented and, unable even to tell whether one is flying the right way up or not, one can easily dive into the ground or pull the plane back so steeply that it stalls. With the instruments going round and round I knew for sure that I was in deep trouble so I took what I thought was the only possible solution: I closed the throttle and let the plane "do its own thing." At least I still knew which way was down. As soon as she came out of cloud and I could see the landscape, I levelled out. Had I been flying lower or if the cloud base had been on the ground, I should not be here to tell the tale.

In 1965 I took over mobile medicine among the Masai, which up to now had been looked after by Roy Schaeffer. The Masai were our most difficult patients because they were reluctant to accept our help and treatments. They are an arrogant tribe, entrenched in their own traditions with no desire at all to join the twentieth century, proud of a past in which they dominated by reason of their bravery and military organization. Numbering some 250,000, divided between Kenya and Tanzania, they are the second largest of the nomad tribes after the Somalis. Their territory is shaped like an hour-glass, with the frontier—not that they pay the least attention to it—running through the middle.

The early colonial governments in Kenya chose not to force unwanted medical services on the Masai; it was felt best to leave them alone, content with their traditional customs and medicines. After Independence, however, Tanzania no longer sought help from Kenyan doctors, but Kenya decided it should do something for its own Masai, and asked AMREF to take this on. Roy Schaeffer had begun working in Arusha, Tanganyika, and in the Masai plains, and started the mobile units in the early days of AMREF. Born and brought up among the Masai by his missionary parents, he spoke the language fluently. They respected and accepted him as a "blood brother" and nicknamed him "Bakooma," meaning "he who never rests." It soon became clear to me that if we wanted to get close to the Masai it was vital to speak their language. If not, we would lose all credibility and be completely shut out. I myself learned only a few words, but I made sure that our team consisted of Masai medical assistants and drivers, plus two English nurses who had learned the language.

First to come to us were the women and children, and then the elderly; younger men were more hesitant but eventually they began to come as well. Clinics, incidentally, could never start before 10 a.m. when milking was finished. We had converted the last of Michael Wood's lorries for a trailer pulled by a Land-Rover, which we used as a mobile dispensary. The Masai, despite their renowned agility, seemed to have some difficulty in climbing the three or four steps up to it; at first they were very wary and surprisingly clumsy—steps were something outside their experience.

One of our very first tasks was to find sites for a school and a static dispensary. The first requirement was a well, the second some Somali *dukas*, because the Somalis always set up shop in places likely to develop in future. These traders provided us with valuable information on local life and customs and the state of mind of the nomadic Masai. Once we had taken all these matters into consideration we were then able to discuss the pros and cons of where to build a landing strip.

We were well aware that it was not going to be easy to get the Masai to accept Western medicine, so we trod very cautiously, drumming up support and recommendations from every source we could to gain their trust. Charles Winnington-Ingram, a former neighbour of mine at Ol Kalou, who had learned to speak their language from his Masai herdsmen, was a great help in all this. He had made friends with the Kangere, a Masai clan living near Kajiado. Through one of them he heard that the *laigwanani*, or chief, had been speared in the thigh in a little inter-clan difference of opinion.

Tipped off by Winnington-Ingram, Michael Wood went off to see the Kangere chief, and found his wound was quite serious as his sciatic nerve had been severed. Wood operated to repair the nerve, and three months later his patient was walking again—he even learned to drive a tractor—and the only permanent damage was loss of nearly all sensation in one foot. For this he had thereafter always to wear sandals in the bush to protect it from injury.

After the success of this operation, the Kangere welcomed us enthusiastically. They invited us to visit them and offered us their mead, a sweet drink with unusually insidious effects: you don't feel at all tipsy and your head remains clear, but when you try to get up your legs have turned to jelly. The friendship and confidence shown us by this clan was the open sesame we needed to the rest of the Masai, and from that time on AMREF was known and respected. At last we had hold of the thread with which to weave our healing web. We were careful to consult the Masai when setting our landing strips. Once they had given the time and the sweat of their brows to clear a strip they regarded it as their property, guarded and maintained it, and kept their herds off it.

The Masai have many fine qualities but one of the greatest is that they never rescind a decision once it has been taken. They are also very democratic and any decision has to have the approval of the whole clan. The matter under discussion will be argued as long as is necessary to convince everyone and reach unanimity, and after that no one is allowed second thoughts.

Little by little my team shaped up. Danieli, the driver, who was also our mechanic and my interpreter, helped with such tasks as putting drops in children's eyes. The two English nurses who spoke Masai were Rosemary and Robbie (the latter's real name was Winifred Robinson). They spent two weeks in the bush with the mobile unit, and in the third week I joined them and we took off by plane to hold "flight clinics" in places inaccessible by road.

Before I took over from Roy Schaeffer he helped me take part in an interesting study on the Masai. George Mann, an American nutrition specialist, had asked us a number of questions on the eating habits of the Masai. How was it that a tribe who lived solely on milk and blood only very rarely suffer from heart disease? He wanted, forgive the pun, to get to the heart of the matter, and was relying on us to introduce him to these extraordinary warriors whose diet, by Western standards, should have killed them, but remained perfectly healthy, with normal cholesterol levels.

Professor Mann had brought with him an alarming device, a kind of mini-escalator driven by a small petrol motor. With Schaeffer standing by as interpreter, he tested Masai males of all ages on his treadmill. They had to climb onto the escalator and to run as hard and fast as they could. Old and young alike were subjected to these tests, which they took in good part, running at full pelt and laughing and joking all the while. They beat Olympic records without any sign of fatigue and seemed highly diverted by this new game. The specialist examining the "athletes" after the tests grew ever more perplexed.

When Mann went home, the second part of the program remained to be carried out. This consisted of collecting Masai hearts post-mortem. This presented no particular problem since the tribe attach no importance to corpses, which they abandon quite unceremoniously. I was in charge of this operation and I issued health officials at the Kajiado, Narok, Kilgoris and Kisii clinics with the instruments necessary for the job. They were given saws and shears to cut through ribs and I paid them for this rather macabre task. In all we collected fifty hearts; one was from a female and had to be rejected as the study was confined to men—more liable, poor creatures, to heart disease than us women. I then put the hearts in metal flasks of formalin and posted them off to Professor Mann at Nashville University, Tennessee. We had no official authorization to carry on this kind of commerce, so for Customs purposes we labelled the packages "Used personal effects." This, after all, was no less than the truth.

George Mann found, once he had received and studied the specimens, that these were enormously strong hearts with great big coronary arteries that no amount of atheroma was likely to block. Their constant physical exercise and frequent long journeys more than compensated for any deficiency in their diet. I imagine that this particular study, which gained wide publicity in the States, may have been an important factor in the current fashion in the West for jogging.

The Masai are subject to trachoma due to the masses of flies that buzz around them. Living as they do, close to their cattle, in small, poorly ventilated huts covered with cow dung, also makes them prone to respiratory infections. The disease that worries them most, however, is gonorrhoea, which in women leads to sterility. This is a disaster for the Masai, for whom children represent both capital and insurance. It was largely our success in curing gonorrhoea that helped us to overcome their resistance to modern medicine. News of our first successes in curing this infection and restoring fertility to our patients spread rapidly and convinced others that there was something in what we had to offer.

In the thirty years since AMREF's flying doctors first took to the air, they have had very few accidents. Is this clean slate due to luck, prudence or skill? It is probably a mixture of all three. At all events it confirms our basic premise, that in Kenya the air is safer than the roads.

We have had only one fatal accident, though that is one too many. On 14 April 1973, the Foundation notified Michael Wood at his home at Ol Molog that one of our planes was overdue at Dodoma, in central Tanzania. The pilot had last made contact at Dosidosi, a largish village in the south-east of the Masai steppe. From there he had taken off to fly east to Kijungu but had never arrived.

Miles Burton, the pilot of the overdue plane, was a young white Kenyan; the plane was a single-engined Cessna 206 that had just been serviced in Nairobi—we did not then have our own maintenance facilities. On that particular day I was with the Woods at Ol Molog, having called in on my way back from a clinic at Moshi, and the news that the plane was missing threw us all into a state of extreme anxiety. We could only speculate on what might have happened to Miles in this largely uninhabited area—perhaps he had been taken ill and forced to put down in the bush. We contacted the airport at Kilimanjaro, which could give us no information. We then called the police who sent out an SOS. Some hours later they called us back:

"We have received a message from the police post at Kibaya that some local Masai say they saw a plane come down not far from a *manyatta*."

Kibaya is a village a little north of Dosidosi. There was no doubt that the plane that had "fallen out of the sky" was ours. At dawn the following day, we took off from Ol Molog for Kibaya, a hundred and fifty miles south. When we arrived, the police put a Land-Rover at our disposal and we drove off with some Masai who knew the site of the crash. It was tough going, first on a rough track and then hacking our way through thick bush. The journey was so slow going that we were still not there by nightfall.

We calculated that the plane must have come down on the Thursday. We had been alerted on Friday, and it was now Saturday night. We tried to keep our hopes up but we were not really very optimistic. There was a full moon and we decided to leave the vehicle and to continue our search on foot. An hour later we reached the *manyatta*. The villagers dashed our last hopes.

"We have found the plane. It is about twenty minutes from here, but there is no point in your going tonight. It caught fire and the pilot is dead."

We spent the night in the open air, sleeping on the ground. By dawn we were on our way. We crawled along a path, little more than a tunnel, the Masai had cut through the dense, almost impenetrable bush, studded with thorny acacia trees. The Cessna had crashed into this tangle of vegetation. The front half of the plane was burnt to a cinder, the rear was almost intact. We found the books Miles had taken with him, but nothing was left of him but his head and torso.

From the moment the Masai warriors had discovered the crashed plane they had mounted guard in relays around the wrecked machine to prevent wild animals from profaning what was left of Miles's body. According to them, the plane had exploded in the air before diving into the ground. If the pilot had still been conscious, he would probably have tried to put the plane down on the flat tops of the acacia trees to soften the impact.

There was nothing we could do except go back to Kibaya and on home until the police and Civil Aviation officials had completed their investigations, which took several days. When it was over I flew down to bring the body back to Nairobi. The Masai made a litter and helped me to carry Miles Burton's mortal remains to the Land-Rover and put them in a body bag. All that was left of the cheerful young man whom we had all known and liked was stowed in the small forward locker in my plane.

The inquest confirmed the Masai's reports. The metal fuel pipe to the inlet manifold showed two cracks, one small and old, and a second, larger, new crack that had caused the final break. We discovered that Miles Burton had been uneasy about making this trip at all: he was not happy about the plane's performance and had complained that the engine was still misfiring even after its recent service. The mechanics had missed the cracks in the pipe that interfered with the fuel supply.

It was then possible to reconstruct the accident. On Thursday, 13 June, at about 10 a.m., Miles had landed and then taken off again from Dosidosi. The runway was bumpy and in very bad condition, and this had clearly been the cause of the second fracture. The engine began to falter as he tried to climb away and, thinking something had gone wrong with the fuel pump, he had switched on the emergency electric pump, increasing the leak of fuel over the engine and red-hot exhaust manifold causing an explosion setting the engine and cabin on fire. We expressed our gratitude to the Masai for their help with a gift of three cows. They had behaved splendidly from start to finish of the tragedy, and without them we should never have found the wreckage or poor Miles's remains. I flew over the scene of the crash and even flying very low found it was impossible to see through the acacia tree canopy.

People who fly with me for the first time inevitably ask the same question: "Flying as much as you do, to the most inaccessible places, how come you have never had an accident?" I am convinced that most people find it amazing that planes stay up. They imagine, whether consciously or subconsciously, that a machine that is heavier than air will hurtle back to Planet Earth at the first opportunity. It is no use trying to tell them that the figures prove beyond doubt that planes offer by far the safest mode of transport, and a complete waste of time to tell them that even if your engine fails you can still glide a distance equal to six times the height at which you are flying, which leaves you a comfortable margin in which to pick somewhere to land without too much damage, particularly if you are over the desert. Consequently, the higher a plane flies, the safer it is. The main hazard for a ship is the coast; for a plane it is the ground. If I fly at fifty feet over the roof of a house, bystanders will say I am a daredevil, but the same people would not move a muscle if while driving they passed another car with only a yard to spare. Yet if each vehicle is travelling at 75 m.p.h. the collision speed would be 150 m.p.h. and, unlike a plane, neither vehicle on the road has another dimension in which to escape—so who then is the daredevil?

The main danger is from wild animals dashing out of the bush and onto the runway just as one is trying to land. Not only do we have to contend with wild animals but also with cows and goats that have given their herdsmen the slip. A dog was responsible for smashing the retractable undercarriage of my present plane, which is much more fragile than a fixed undercarriage. The strut gave way, the wing gave way and that was that. The dog was dead, I was desolate.

Another time at Oloika, near Shombole in the Rift Valley, I had just landed and was still rolling very fast when a giraffe dashed out of a grove of trees. I did not have enough room to take off again so a collision seemed inevitable. At the very last second the giraffe stopped on the edge of the runway. We stared deep into one another's eyes and then, averting her gaze, she stalked slowly back to the forest. Recently, a zebra dashed into the path of one of our twin-engined planes. The unfortunate animal was hit by the propeller of the port engine, and the sudden obstruction damaged the engine beyond repair. Our chief pilot, Jim Heather-Hayes, was philosophical about the mishap.

"Even without the prang the engine needed replacing. It had reached the end of its useful life."

Michael Wood used to tell of a short—though not as short as he would have liked—encounter with a rhinoceros.

"I was just about to land when I saw the animal standing bang in the middle of the runway. I opened the throttle and hedge-hopped several times in the hope of making the huge beast move away. I managed to get him to trundle to the end of the runway while I landed, but no sooner had I done so than the rhino trotted up to investigate this noisy invasion.

"I had no idea what to do next. Luckily I hadn't stopped the engine; I gunned it and the noise stopped the animal in its tracks, but as soon as I cut back the engine it advanced again. As he came closer I decided that the best means of defence was attack, so I taxied the plane towards him. I would have liked to blow the horn but these are not standard equipment in a plane.

Instead, I yelled, 'Get out of the way, you big brute,' but my voice was drowned by the noise of the engine. Eventually the rhino got bored or scared by my manoeuvring, and trotted off in a huff. At that precise moment I was greatly relieved to see the car being sent for me arriving in a cloud of dust. I hopped out of the plane and into the car, hoping that the rhino would not return for a closer look."

Happy were the days, such minor inconveniences apart, before nearly all the rhino population had been massacred. Today a few are still to be found in the game reserves but they have often had to be imported from countries less ravaged by poachers than Kenya, and they are watched over by armed guards. The rhino is a formidable beast, a prehistoric tank that can slice through the sheet metal of a plane or of a tourist minibus. Wild boar, anteaters, termites and ants all dig deep holes hidden by the grass. These are difficult to detect, as I discovered when I was taxiing along slowly to line up for take-off at Mkunumbi, near Lamu. My undercarriage sank into the earth and was literally swallowed up, while the propeller turned into a plough. Even those responsible for the upkeep and maintenance of the strips can have no idea where yawning underground cavities may have developed. These are minor incidents so long as they do not cause injury, but they are extremely annoying when they cause delay on an urgent call, and in time and money they are costly, particularly for an organization such as ours with limited funds. This is why we never stop trying to make certain that those responsible for maintaining our landing strips inspect them regularly, cut the grass and clear all obstacles.

Africans have many excellent qualities, but interest in preventive maintenance and routine work is not among them, and planes no longer surprise or amaze them. They have seen so many landings without incident that they do not always understand the need to keep the strips clear at all times. On the other hand they respond magnificently to a challenge. I have known a thousand-yard airstrip carved out of the bush in a single day by a team of nine hundred men! The radio is our most valuable asset—we never take off without receiving radio confirmation that the strip on which we propose landing has been inspected and is in good order.

Sometimes the human machine lets us down. Some months ago I was just finishing my clinic at a little island on the Somalia border. It was late afternoon and I had been sitting on a low stool for a considerable time. When I tried to get up I felt a terrible pain in my right knee—I had torn a cartilage. My leg would not support me, and trying to walk was agony. It was the worst possible timing. I absolutely had to be in Lamu before nightfall, and to do that I had to leave Kiwayu by boat and get to Mokokoni, where my plane was waiting. Helped by Ali, my nurse at Lamu, I managed to stagger down the cliff to the boat. I then hobbled somehow to the jeep that was to take me to the plane. The problem I still had to solve was how to pilot it with only one useful leg?

In a plane one's feet control the rudder with two pedals, which allow one to turn right or left. Once airborne this control is not essential, since one can perfectly well turn the plane, somewhat inelegantly, by banking it with the joystick. On the ground, however, the rudder bar controls the nose wheel and there is no other way to steer. For take-off and landing I needed the help of another foot.

I had myself carried to my seat and promoted Ali to co-pilot. All planes, even the smallest, are equipped with dual control. Ali had been flying with me for years and was familiar with the controls. We quickly agreed on a way of dealing with my predicament. "You put your foot on the right pedal. I'll take care of the left one. When we move, if we want to go right, I'll tell you when to press on your pedal. Is that understood?" This extraordinary partnership worked perfectly. Poor Ali was torn between amusement and anxiety, but he reacted magnificently to my commands.

"Press harder—let go—press again—hold that—let go."

Taxiing to the end of the runway gave Ali time to adjust himself to his unusual situation and practise what I had just told him. I lined up for take-off and opened the throttle. Ali gave a little sigh, and off we went, up, up, up and away over the sea. I was so absorbed in this novel way of taking off that I quite forgot the pain in my knee; this, however, returned a little while later in full force. The flight to Lamu seemed to take an eternity.

This adventure reminds me of a much more dramatic one involving two young students in Turkana, a German and a Kenyan-born Indian. They were taking supplies by Land-Rover up to a University of Nairobi expedition. On the return journey they stopped their vehicle to allow a big herd of cattle to get by. As they sat waiting, a bullet whizzed through the car's upholstery, tore into the driver's right arm and then through the passenger's left arm and his leg. The shot had been fired by one of a gang of *shiftas* who thought the khaki-coloured Land-Rover was an army vehicle driven by soldiers. When they realized their mistake, they ran away, leaving their victims in a bad way.

The students were resourceful young men and rather than sit waiting for help that might never come, they got under way again in spite of the pain, one steering with his left hand, while the other used his right hand to change gear. In this way they managed to drive to the District Commissioner's office, where they were given first aid. We were sent for and the next day, accompanied by another pilot, I came to fetch the wounded pair. We landed on an old disused military airstrip at Sigor. It was overgrown with weeds and tunnelled by termites, and we came to a stop about eighteen inches from a three-foot anthill a concrete-like pillar quite invisible in the thick undergrowth.

Taking off from what resembled an obstacle course needed careful thought. The District Commissioner mobilized a team to cut down the biggest branches. He then draped his shirt over a bush to give us a marker for take-off, and to pinpoint the anthills exactly we asked a Turkana to stand on top of each one. Having made these unusual but effective arrangements, we took off without mishap and flew to Nairobi with the two casualties on mattresses in the back of the plane.

Fate never warns us what she has in store. One day I had just taken off from Witu, near Lamu, when one of my passengers said quietly, "Doctor, something is dangling under the plane. Might it be anything dangerous?" The undercarriage had mysteriously hooked up the wire from a fence, and carried it aloft. I realized immediately that the dangling wire cable could spell disaster if it got in the way of our next landing or got tangled up in the under-carriage. I flew on but touched down at Lamu as gently as if I were landing a crate of eggs.

All bush pilots have a store of such anecdotes about their mis-adventures. The fact remains, however, that there is rarely a mishap at any of the hundred or so landing strips we use throughout the year. Certain strips are flooded during the long rains, which is why I take my holidays at that time of year, when many of the clinics I service are impossible to reach.

We are not all ace pilots and we don't clock up a vast number of flying hours, as our particular kind of work calls for short hops. On the other hand, we land and take-off many times a day, and are thoroughly familiar with the landing strips and their particular snags. We operate rather differently from most professional pilots and when they join us they have to learn our ways. On my first mission for AMREF I was told to take Captain Travers with me. He was an instructor from Nakuru who had flown all his life and had clocked up an astronomical number of flying hours, something like forty thousand I believe. I imagine that my superiors feared that, novice that I was, I might get lost or smash up my plane on the makeshift runways. It was not I, however, but the experienced Captain Travers who muffed a landing, missed the runway and damaged the undercarriage of my plane.

The other side of the coin is that we bush pilots are not always at ease in great international airports where complicated procedures are required, and their vigilant and omnipresent air traffic controllers are not always impressed with our flair and improvisation. The first time I flew into Aden is not an occasion I care to boast about. I had come to visit the Besses and had already touched down at Addis Ababa and Djibouti. It was one of my first long flights, and I was not yet hardened to the fatigue from the concentration required for the journey. The flight over the sea had seemed interminable, and I had a splitting headache. The sun seemed red-hot and the heat was intense. I was wearing dark glasses, which distorted distances. Aden's airport was enormous and the traffic non-stop; jets were landing and taking off constantly, and the control tower hassled me to get into the traffic pattern. I found it impossible to estimate my height above the enormous runway, and in my confusion throttled back too quickly. The plane dropped, bounced and did a nose-dive, and the propeller hit the tarmac. I had to send the prop to Rhodesia for repair, which took ten days.

I was lucky to escape lightly from this accident, but it taught me, novice as I was, a sharp lesson. An accident is always the result of a chain of unfavourable circumstances. In this particular case it was a combination of fatigue, lack of concentration, the harrassment of the control tower and my lack of experience in landing at international airports. Since then I have always tried to remember that it is only by knowing one's limitations that one survives to become an "old" pilot.

I kept my first plane, the Piper Cherokee 235 I bought in May 1964, until 1970. I was very attached to this machine, registered as Alpha Alpha Lima. It was my first plane, and had seen my debut as a pilot—that memorable flight to Europe and back. But I needed a more powerful engine for taking off with heavy loads from short, hot, high-altitude runways. So I traded up to a Cherokee 6, Alpha Juliet Echo, with a fixed undercarriage but with a much more powerful engine and with a variable-pitch propeller.

Finally, in 1975, I acquired my current plane, Alpha Zulu Tango, a Cherokee Lance, which with its retractable undercarriage is faster and more powerful than either of my two previous planes. Despite its twenty years it is still equal to the task and is carefully maintained and serviced in our workshops. I have not bought another plane mainly for reasons of economy. In the past twenty years the world recession has greatly increased the price of planes and fuel. Also I don't believe I could better my current plane. There appears to have been little or no change in the technical development of light planes, at least in those available to an individual or an organization such as ours, with a very limited budget.

The lack of progress in this particular field poses a number of problems. The design of the engines has not changed, they are heavy on fuel. They need specially refined aviation fuel, which is extremely expensive and getting more and more difficult to obtain. One might think helicopters would be suitable for our work, but on the one hand these are infinitely more sophisticated, cost the earth to run, and need frequent services and replacement of vital parts; on the other, they are unsuited to our particular kind of work because of their short range.

So, imperfect as it may be, the light plane is still the best means of transport in Africa. Thanks to my machine I was able to take part in a marvellous scientific mission, the French Omo expedition. This paleolithic research expedition, organized and carried out by the French National Research Council (CNRS) between 1966 and 1976, completely revolutionized our knowledge of the origins of the human species.

Early in June 1969 I was a guest at a party given at the French Embassy in Nairobi in honour of the members of this mission, who were preparing to leave on their third expedition. Among the guests was an old acquaintance, Christian Zuber, whom I had known as a young man in Mulhouse. Like me, he came from a Swiss family who had settled in Alsace. The Zubers lived close to us, in the rue du Jura. Later I met Christian again. By that time he had become a writer and film producer, and was the author of the famous series *Camera at the Ready*. He often came to Kenya and was a regular guest at Subukia; sometimes I accompanied him on his trips.

Zuber introduced me to Yves Coppens, site director of the dig. It did not take him long to tell me, with characteristically passionate enthusiasm and verve, about the work then being undertaken by his team in the remote desert region near where the river Omo empties into Lake Turkana. Seeing how interested I was in this project he invited me to visit the site. I gladly accepted and asked for precise details on the location of the dig, which Coppens was unable to give me.

"It's near a small town called Kalam and a village called Duss.

But there's a plane that will bring us fresh supplies from Nairobi on a regular basis. Have a word with the pilot. He'll be able to tell you exactly where our camp is."

I got in touch with the young pilot at once. I used to meet him from time to time at Wilson Airport—he worked for Wilken, the Piper agents. He was anything but helpful. He told me he touched down at Kibbish Wells on the Ethiopian border. I knew that this was impossible, so I did not press for any further information. I realized that the last thing he wanted was for me and my plane to visit what he considered to be *his* clients at the dig. Flying to and from the site was a lucrative business he and his boss intended to keep for themselves. They had no intention of letting a third party muscle in on their territory, even if only for a friendly visit.

To make certain of finding the site, I made a pact with Zuber. Immediately after his arrival at the dig he would write me a letter, giving full details of its location. He did this, and even wrote a second letter, both of which he gave to the pilot. Finally, Christian sent me an ordinary postcard couched in code, which the pilot did deliver to me. He obviously had no idea of what it was about. The card gave me a complete and exact itinerary. I was to fly over Lake Turkana and the mouth of the Omo and then north, following the river for twenty minutes. I would find the camp on the right bank.

From Subukia I would have about three hundred miles to fly, which would be two and a half hours' flying time, or three if I allowed half an hour for contingencies. I made certain I had plenty of fuel. The tanks were full, and I stowed two extra jerricans in the hold; this I calculated would get me there and back in case I could not refuel on the return journey. Having sufficient reserves of fuel when flying in Africa becomes an obsession.

To save fuel I flew high over Lake Turkana and the Omo River. In fact, I flew so high that I missed the camp. I realized my mistake when I reached the place where the river makes a great loop to the south-east. I had flown too far, and there was nothing for it but to double back. This time I flew low over the valley and soon, to my relief, saw the runway below. I flew over it a couple of times to signal my arrival, then landed. A car sent by the French mission was waiting for me.

Yves Coppens and his wife Françoise greeted me warmly and showed me round their domain. A number of big tents had been set up on top of a plateau to house the expedition's workforce. In addition there was a laboratory, a mess tent and a kitchen. Everything was perfectly organized. There was even a water-treatment system. The red, thick, heavily silted river water was poured into two forty-gallon drums; alum was added to precipitate the sediment, after which the water went through a series of filters. This took care of the vital problem—in such a remote spot—of providing safe drinking water and was just one example of the well-planned infrastructure of the camp.

Each year, from June to September, the organizers had to plan their expedition and make certain that living conditions for fifty people in the camp were as comfortable as possible. In addition to the scientific teams working on the dig, there were Ethiopian and Kenyan colleagues as well as civil servants, policemen and a regular flow of visitors.

Françoise Coppens ran the camp and the commissariat with admirable efficiency. The food was good and the wine excellent. Morale among the team was high and they clearly enjoyed working together. They had to work hard, however: the researchers and their teams of assistants left for the site at dawn, came back for lunch at noon, then worked all afternoon in the heat, returning to base around 6 p.m. They worked these long hours to make the most of the short equatorial days and the short working season.

The site had come about by a freak geological accident, a large 3,500-foot-high rock fall stretching from the plateau the camp was on down to the river and exposing ancient fossil beds rather like a vanilla slice cut obliquely. Coppens compared this phenomenon to the slanted edge of a book, allowing one to leaf through millions of years of the world's history at leisure. Seen from above, the layers of strata looked like a flight of stairs and were spectacular. Coloured white, red, black and grey they made a perfect abstract painting.

This site in the lower valley of the Omo, with its important fossil deposits, had long been of interest to scholars. At night, by the light of the campfire, Coppens would entertain me with the story of the Vicomte Du Bourg de Bozas, who as the result of an unhappy love affair decided to cross Africa from the Red Sea to the Atlantic. Leaving Djibouti in 1901 he reached the region of the Omo in the spring of 1902. He was accompanied by a Dr. Brumpt, a naturalist who, marvelling at his good fortune in finding such an exposed geological treasure trove, collected a first harvest of fossils: animal bones, the remains of fish, teeth and bits of ivory.

Du Bourg de Bozas never finished his journey: he died of malaria some months later on the banks of the Oubangi River. Brumpt returned to France with his specimens from the Omo, which aroused such great interest among archeologists and paleontologists that Professor Camille Arambourg decided to organize a further expedition. In eight months, in 1932–33, on the site pinpointed by Brumpt, he collected four tons of fossils, which he studied for several years. No human remains were found in his excavations and the expedition might never have come to public notice had it not been for the furore caused by the paleontologist Louis Leakey's discovery of fossilized remains of hominids far older than any so far known in Kenya and Tanzania.

In 1966 Emperor Haile Selassie, on an official visit to Nairobi, was astonished and mortified to learn that no such prestigious ancestors had been discovered in his country, which bordered that in which Leakey had made such astonishing finds. The Negus, always anxious to proclaim the grandeur and antiquity of his people, told Leakey he hoped that similar fossils might be found in Ethiopia. His remark did not fall on deaf ears. Leakey told the Emperor that the remains found in the Omo were very similar to those of the 600,000-year-old "Nutcracker Man" he had found during his first dig at Olduvai Gorge in Tanzania. Working a similar dig in Ethiopia might well, he said, result in the finding of even older ancestors of man.

Leakey's optimistic assessment was exactly what the Emperor had hoped to hear and he immediately asked Leakey to mount an international expedition. By 1967 Leakey had assembled three impressive teams of Kenyan, American and French specialists, ready and willing to start work.

The French team was led by Camille Arambourg, who was already familiar with the site, and Yves Coppens, the aged professor's protégé, to whom he had passed on much of his scientific knowledge. Master and pupil had travelled together in Algeria, and Coppens had already carried out research in Chad. The French team was therefore in expert hands. The Kenyan team, led by Louis Leakey and his son Richard, was no less prestigious. Leakey was responsible for adding a new dimension to paleontology and his son was to follow admirably in his famous father's footsteps. The American team, directed by Professor Clark Howell, set themselves up near the French and the two camps shared the little airstrip. There was some jostling and rivalry for position but, on the whole, the two teams got on well and were helpful to one another. As ever, the Americans were superbly equipped, and generously shared their powerful radio, which made possible communications between the Omo and Addis Ababa or Nairobi.

The Kenyans had chosen a site some distance away from the other teams. Perhaps it did not come up to their expectations, or perhaps they thought they might do better in their own country. Whatever the reasons, they abandoned their site in 1968, well into their second year, and took themselves off to the banks of Lake Turkana at Koobi Fora. It proved to be an inspired decision. Soon after beginning work there, the Leakeys made their stupendous find—the remains of *Homo habilis*, who had lived two and a half million years ago.

Yves Coppens is now so famous there is no need for me to expatiate on his expertise and charisma, but at the site at Omo I was able to appreciate at first hand his talents as a leader and organizer. He was punctilious over detail, and regarded the welfare and safety of his team as of paramount importance. One evening, one of our cars had not returned to base. They were all equipped with a radio, but not a sound had been heard from this particular vehicle. Coppens decided to go and look for the missing car, and I asked to go with him. He drove slowly and with some difficulty—great care was necessary to avoid over-turning—down the steep purpose-built track that zigzagged through the various archeological layers. Yves was haunted by the idea of an accident waiting to happen. He would often say: "It is far more important to me to get my team home alive and well than to obtain scientific results, no matter how exciting." Halfway down the slope we met the missing team on their way home. They had worked late on the dig and hadn't switched on their radio so were quite unaware of the anxiety caused by their absence. Coppens was so relieved to see them that nothing more was said.

Meanwhile Christian Zuber was filming everything that moved. He had no shortage of subjects, as the river banks teemed with wildlife. Towards nightfall, clouds of little birds called koleas descended on the fields to feed. They were so numerous that they completely obscured the setting sun. The peasants stood guard and tried, with little success, to drive them off.

The Omo is infested by crocodiles and no one in their senses would bathe in it, but a few foolhardy Americans stripped off and went in. One of them was taken by a crocodile and when the local fishermen later killed the creature, they found part of an arm and a leg in its stomach.

Christian Zuber had a frightening experience. One morning, as Françoise Coppens came out of her tent to clean her teeth she came face to face with a cobra that had been attracted to the camp by a little hare, a gift from the Dassenech labourers. The snake glided away between the rocks, with Christian in hot pur-suit, his camera at the ready. When he found the snake, it spat two jets of venom straight into his eyes. The pain was terrible and he was blind for two days. He was also extremely vexed at having forgotten that among the seven or eight species of cobra there is one that spits.

During his first expedition to Omoin 1932, Camille Arambourg had found no trace of hominid remains, but on returning to the dig many years later, he was confident of finding the ancestor of man. The competition between the three scientific missions to be first to find traces of ancestral man was keen.

"You have the *baraka* [luck]," Arambourg told Coppens. "You will find what you are searching for."

His prophecy came true during the very first expedition. On 7 July, 1967, Coppens came back to camp with two pieces of mandible he had just unearthed.

"I showed them to Professor Arambourg, who examined them in silence. Then he fitted the two together, murmuring 'Primates.' Seconds later he muttered 'Anthropomorphe,' and then, his eyes alight with joy, he exclaimed, 'Australopithecus!'"

This was probably the most exciting moment of his life. He had been waiting for thirty-five years for this discovery. When I first met Arambourg he was well into his third visit to the site. In spite of his great age, he was as enthusiastic as ever. There was nothing he enjoyed more than flying over the layers of stratified sediment in a helicopter, and in spite of the fact that it was hard going, he insisted on being present at every dig. His warmth and dignity reminded me of my father. And his courage and endurance were all the more remarkable because he was already seriously ill. He died at the age of eighty-two a few months after returning to France. Yves Coppens took over sole responsibility for the mission at Omo for the next seven years.

Each summer until 1972 I visited Omo. I brought them supplies of fresh vegetables from my garden, which were a welcome addition to their ordinary fare. Whenever Coppens wanted something from Nairobi he would send me a message via the Americans' radio. On my second trip a young pilot anxious to get his flying hours up came with me. I showed him the route and let him get used to the somewhat substandard strip and the frequently difficult crosswind. Later, when I was too busy or on holiday in France I allowed my young friend to use my plane and help out at Omo when they needed him. The Wilken pilot went on flying there, though I dare say a little less often than he would have liked; I never tried to stop him earning his living.

One September I was asked to go to Kalam to see to the repair of a Land-Rover and to take two archeologists to Lake Stephanie, where it was thought there were layers and deposits even older than those at Omo. I left Nairobi with a very full load: five passengers—a nephew, a mechanic and the two researchers—a tool kit, a cylinder head and two jerricans of fuel. Luckily, I still had that reliable old workhorse Juliet Echo. After a very long take-off run we climbed slowly, banking only gently, then descending over the Rift Valley. With such a load there was no question of flying at altitude.

Three and a half hours later we reached Kalam, the nearest town to the expedition site, which had a runway big enough to take a DC3, close to a Protestant mission run by Pastor Swart, an American Baptist. We repaired the Land-Rover, and I flew the two scientists round Lake Stephanie, which apparently did not seem to them very promising. Then I went back to spend the night with the Swarts, an exceptional couple. He was a skilled mechanic with a fully equipped workshop and thus often asked to repair expedition vehicles, and he and his wife had managed to build a school, a hospital and a church despite very scarce resources. The Swarts had already done excellent work in the Sudan before being asked to leave. They had no better luck in Ethiopia: no sooner had the Emperor been deposed, in 1974, than the police arrived at the Swarts' house.

"You have two hours to pack. You may take two suitcases each. You will then get out."

The Swarts took refuge at Ileret, one of my stopovers on Lake Turkana, so I was able to go on seeing them. Here, undaunted, they built a new house and started their missionary activities again. Many of their Ethiopian friends used to come from Kalam, which was only a day away, to visit them. After a few months their activities upset Mengistu's men, and a complaint was made to the Kenya government. Although Ethiopia was now communist the Kenya government still wanted to be on good terms with them, and once again the Swarts were peremptorily asked to evangelize elsewhere, as far from the Ethiopian border as possible. They moved to another part of Kenya for a time and then eventually returned to the States. The departure of such an outstanding couple was Africa's loss; their only crime was to be American missionaries.

I must admit I was far more useful to the French mission as a liaison agent than as a doctor. In fact they had no need of my medical skills as the camp was swarming with medics, all eminent specialists of one kind or another. There were parasitologists, epidemiologists and virologists who for years had been studying animal and insect life, and taking blood samples from the local population. They were fortunate in having such a unique and unspoilt research environment protected from interference by its remoteness. Coppens wanted other scientists to take advantage of such a unique site with the infrastructure he had built up, and gradually the paleontologists, geologists and professors of prehistory were joined by entomologists, ethnologists and even specialists in the study of pollen; these last went by the charming name of palynologists. When all these great minds were gathered together in the mess the table talk was on the highest intellectual level and I learned a great deal. Of course, I don't remember everything I heard, but in my own field I do recollect hearing about the discovery of a new type of plasmodium in the blood of a rodent, something intermediate between the agent of piroplasmosis and the malaria plasmodium. A number of laboratories are studying this new discovery in the hope of making a new vaccine. A new species of flea was also discovered, and promptly named *Xenopsylla coppensis*. Yves Coppens, who has a well-developed sense of humour, says some of his colleagues still ask him whether he is carrying his personal flea.

There were no health problems when I was at the camp. Thanks to the excellent organization and the clean water, the highest standards of hygiene were maintained. I made sure the team took preventive measures against malaria, rife in this area. The population of Omo were less fortunate, for they, like the Turkana, were badly infected with hydatid disease. I made one most interesting observation, however. The local tribes, known as the Boumi or the Nyangatom, lived primitively in a hostile environment, some relying on agriculture, staying in their river village, while others went off into the desert and led a nomadic life with their cattle. These two groups, although closely related members of the same tribe, in many cases brother and sister, developed totally different diseases depending on which lifestyle they followed. Moreover, the children of the farming families, brought up on sorghum and corn, were subject to nutritional deficiencies, while their nomadic relatives living on milk and meat were comparatively healthy. I had already noticed in Kenya that, contrary to general opinion, pastoral nomads live longer than settled farmers.

With each trip I made to the dig I heard the latest instalments of the amazing story the scholars were unearthing. Little by little they deciphered the signs and symbols inscribed in this vast book opened by the chance fault in the side of Africa's great Rift, a volume 3,500 feet thick, recounting page by page four million years of the world's history. Between the "chapters" were layers of ash from the many volcanic eruptions in the Rift Valley over the years, and these made accurate carbon dating possible. Trapped in the sediment were animal fossils, pollens and plants, guides to the evolution of nature. In each epoch it is possible to trace the evolution or disappearance of animal and vegetable species. The pig *Notochoerius andrewsi* quitted the scene when the warthog and the horse made their appearance. *Homo sapiens* was here 3.5 million years ago in his australopithecine form, and with him were found his stone tools, proof positive that here was the oldest prehistoric men ever discovered. Thanks to the Omo and Lake Turkana deposits, Coppens, Leakey and their teams were able to prove that reveille had sounded for mankind a million years earlier than had previously been thought.

Nowadays I look differently at the Rift Valley I have lived in for forty-five years—knowing it was the cradle of humanity makes its magnificent landscapes even more impressive. Also I know there is a lesson to be learned here. As the climate became harsher, primates had to evolve, to sit up, to develop their brains, to organize their survival by means of tools and social structure. It is the necessity of making an effort that has moulded man; it will be sad if this virtue ceases to be in fashion.

I visited the Omo site for the last time in 1972. Until then we had had no problems in crossing the frontier between Ethiopia and Kenya and could come and go as we pleased. The Ethiopians did not object to this Western presence, as it brought employment and fame to an otherwise desolate region on the outskirts of the former Negus's empire.

The digs were more or less equidistant from Nairobi and Addis Ababa, about 450 miles by air and 650 by road. Initially, it seemed logical for the expedition to be based in Nairobi, which offered many advantages. But from 1973, as their country rapidly deteriorated, the Ethiopians insisted that everything should be channelled through Addis and people from Kenya were no longer welcome. Finally, in 1976, Mengistu's communist government put an end to the whole operation. Both the French and the Americans were obliged to leave at a moment's notice, abandoning everything at great financial loss.

Yves Coppens had had his revenge earlier: in 1974 he and Donald Johanson and Maurice Taieb discovered the almost complete skeleton of "Lucy" in the Afar desert, close to Djibouti. The fame of this little australopithecine fossil spread around the world and aroused passionate world interest in a subject hitherto the preserve of scientists, scholars and researchers. Was Lucy an advanced member of an extinct line of apes, just a distant cousin of Man? Or was she already a human being, the reincarnation of Eve, as some liked to see her? Today, Lucy is the Apple of Discord among experts. Should she prove to be Eve, that would be an appropriate name for her. The English expression "bone of contention" is also not inappropriate.

Chapter 5

AN ENDLESS FIGHT

In 1976 Michael Wood asked me to take over the immunization, maternity and child welfare work in the district of Lamu on the Indian Ocean. AMREF had been asked to help because the area was difficult to reach and an aeroplane would be invaluable. The population is spread over a number of small islands and across a narrow coastal strip; links with the outside world are scanty and unreliable. The few tracks around the swamps and mangroves are often cut off by flooding. By plane one can get from Lamu to Kiunga, close to the Somali border, in half an hour. The alternative is a dreadful six-hour journey by road—always supposing one manages to get through what amounts to an obstacle race. A five-minute flight brings one to the island of Pate, a journey that would take two hours by boat, providing the hospital boat had not broken down.

I accepted this new task with pleasure. I was already very attached to Lamu, which I had known for a long time and where I had built a house. Every two months I move from one world into another, three hundred miles and a two-hour flight from Nairobi and spend a week in the "other" Africa—Swahili country, a land with close links to Arabia, with lingering perfumes of India, Indonesia and China.

On leaving Nairobi I fly east over Kamba country and can soon distinguish the characteristic landscape of Machakos. Tremendous effort has been put into trying to develop this particular region and combat the severe erosion of the steep sloping terrain with its soft friable soil. On the terraced hillsides grow coffee plants and fruit trees, from some of which an excellent plum jam is made; the green terraces on the outskirts of Machakos itself bear a slight resemblance to Bali. Sugar cane grows in the valleys, which are dotted with little houses each with its rainwater tank—which AMREF helped to organize—and each village has a small health committee, also inaugurated by us. It is the business of the committee's members to spread the word in each village and explain the importance of having an organized and regular system for conserving water. The result is that the Kamba women no longer have to walk five or ten miles a day to fetch water from a stagnant pool or polluted river. Unlike their neighbours the Kikuyu, the Kamba people, who are deeply attached to their flocks, found it difficult at first to adapt to new methods of agriculture, but nowadays they seem to have come to terms with the new order.

I fly over the Athi River, winding down the foothills of the Yatta Plateau, its waters red with silt from the Highland farms. Finally Mount Mutha marks the end of the well-developed countryside and the start of the featureless savannah that stretches all the way to the distant coast. I am prepared for a boring and monotonous hour flying over the bush, the *nyeka*, the "miles and miles of bloody Africa" descending imperceptibly to the sea.

A stretch of water glitters in the sun. This is Lake Garsen, which marks the Tana basin, at least when the river is full. The setting through which the Tana flows is enormously variable. When it is in flood one might be at the heart of a vast Camargue, and its silt tinges the water red far out to sea—the blood of Africa spreading into the water, flowing from the open wounds in the mountainsides caused by deforestation and erosion. At times of drought, the river is reduced to a trickle, thinned to the point of anorexia as it snakes through the desolate, arid plains.

Lamu comes into sight between the dunes and mangrove swamps. I fly low over miles of beach before reaching the outskirts of the village of Shella, where my house is, and then the big white hospital building and, finally, the roofs and minarets of the town, and the port, full of dhows. There is no need for any other signal of arrival: everyone knows I am here.

I bank right and touch down on the strip on the neighbouring island of Manda, once an ancient coral reef. It was not possible to build a strip at Lamu itself, which is on a sandbank. Once I have landed all I have to do is unload my luggage onto the steaming tarmac and wait for the hospital boat to fetch me. Together with Zanzibar and the old town of Mombasa, Lamu is the last outpost of a civilization that a thousand years ago covered the whole coast of East Africa from Somalia to Mozambique. The word Swahili comes for the Arab *sahel*, which means shore. It refers to both those who live on the coast and their language and culture.

The Swahili people were born of the sea and the wind: climate and geography have formed their history. In this part of the Indian Ocean the monsoon wind, known as the *kaskasi*, blows regularly from the north-east from November to March. From May to September it becomes the *kusi* and blows from the opposite direction. These alternating breezes have made possible a continuous traffic between coastal peoples. Gold, ivory, skins and, above all, slaves torn from Central Africa were exchanged for cotton, silk, spices, glass and porcelain brought from India and the Far East.

The middlemen in this traffic were Arabs from Oman and Muscat. They married black women and put roots down deep along the coast, founding some thirty city-states, at times allied, more often rivals. The mixture of blood created a new and original coloured community whose African exuberance was tempered by the more rigorous customs of Islam. On Lamu there are thirty mosques for twenty thousand inhabitants. One is particularly holy and is the goal of one of the greatest pilgrimages of the Moslem world. In the street the women hide themselves beneath austere black *buibuis*, which make them look like giant spiders, while in their homes they wear colourful, gauzy, shimmering fabrics and spend their days with their friends, decorating their arms and legs with hennaed arabesques and performing dances that would give the most liberal ayatollahs a fit.

After the Omo adventure, Françoise Coppens became an ethnologist, and she produced an interesting description of this fascinating and paradoxical society that owes more to Asia than to

Africa and by its very isolation from the world has preserved for us the customs of the medieval Orient.

The Swahili empire owed its prosperity to that excellent vessel the dhow, with its triangular sail tapering like a gull's wing. Rustic and solid-looking, it nonetheless responds to the lightest breeze. In the Lamu archipelago the dhows evoke a continuous ballet as they weave their way along the channels between the islands. Whatever their business, whether it be fishing, trade or acting as "bus" or taxi, the dhows have been the first to profit from the tourist boom and this may well be why they will survive in Lamu.

Cross-breeding is also visible in Lamu's architecture. The mud huts with roofs thatched with *makuti* palm leaves look more African than do the large houses built of coral. These, with their narrow windows, are more in the style of the Persian Gulf of which this coast was a kind of protectorate. Interior decor and furnishings owe much to India, notably the splendid ornamental canopied beds and the slatted windows, and one often sees rare and beautiful pieces of old Chinese porcelain on the walls.

The fort at Lamu is often thought to have been built by the Portuguese, but in fact it was built by the Sultan of Lamu to defend the town against the Pate people. It was used as a prison for many years but now has been skillfully restored and has become a museum.

Lamu itself is a living museum, if slightly run down since the abolition of slavery, British colonization and the mortal rivalry of Mombasa relegated it to the sidelines. Not the least of its charms is that it missed the bandwagon of Western progress. So perfectly is it emmeshed in the past that it was chosen by the producers of the film *To the Source of the Nile* as a backdrop for scenes shot in what was supposedly Zanzibar in the last century. As TV aerials rising from typical *makuti* roofs were an anachronism, the producers of the film asked their owners to remove them temporarily. They were, of course, paid for the inconvenience, and to show that they had really kept their side of the bargain they arrived on the set with their aerials, where they were given a few dollars and allowed to go. This was a serious mistake, as they simply gave the aerials to friends or relatives, who repeated the procedure. When the film crew totted up their figures they realized that they had paid out for far more aerials than there were TVs in Lamu, if not in the whole district. Next time round they wisely impounded each aerial they paid for until shooting was finished.

The only car allowed in Lamu was the District Commissioner's Land-Rover. The streets of the town are exceedingly narrow and there are no other roads. Apart from dhows, donkeys are the only means of transport. At least three hundred of these charming creatures roam freely through the town when they are being used to carry loads. They amble about happily, from time to time suddenly gathering in groups as if for a committee meeting. Often they seek shelter from the hot sun in the cool arcades of the Arabic-style houses on the seafront. A British animal welfare foundation opened an animal dispensary where the donkeys were regularly inspected, vaccinated and fed. It seems that the local breed of donkey only lives eleven years, compared with the twenty-seven an English donkey may aspire to. Reason enough, one supposes, to try to help them. There are so many of them that, from time to time they cause a public nuisance. I once read in a local paper that a pair of donkeys, chasing one another through the streets, knocked over and trampled a toddler, who lost two teeth. Another animal was stopped for speeding, and detained for a whole afternoon in the police station.

For some time, the town councillors were engaged in serious debate on the vexed question of the over supply of donkey droppings, which they felt did nothing for the narrow, crowded little streets. Their final proposal was to equip the donkeys with nappies, but this project does not seem to have got off the ground, as one might say. What would Lamu be without its donkeys, as much a part of its decor as its swarms of cats, or the more severe and obsequious marabou storks that camp on the rubbish tips at the entrance to the town?

Another odd variety of fauna flourished in Lamu in the late sixties—the hippie, en route to Kathmandu. I imagine they chose to come via Lamu because it was easy to obtain the hashish used throughout the area, rather than for the intrinsic beauty of the place. These hordes have now disappeared but they did not give Lamu a very savoury reputation. From time to time one of these oddballs still turns up, but they tend now to be gold-plated specimens with American Express cards poking out of the pockets of their carefully torn jeans.

I discovered Lamu in 1962. Richard Onslow, one of my farming friends, had just got his pilot's licence and hired a plane, and he and his wife, their small son and I took off on a jaunt. We followed the Athi River as it merged into and became the Sabaki and flowed through Tsavo Park to Malindi and then we turned north and flew up the coast. A season of serious floods was just coming to an end, and the countryside was at its greenest. All the ponds and waterholes were full, and hundreds of elephants were wallowing in the pools or climbing the dunes bordering the ocean. (That was only thirty years ago, but when I fly over this part of the coast today there is no wildlife to be seen, only the shadow of my plane moving across the sand.)

We had taken the precaution of bringing our sleeping bags, because in those days there were no facilities for tourists, who were then very few and far between. The only hotel, Petley's Inn, used mainly by British civil servants, was closed owing to the death of its proprietor. By great good luck I met up with Ba Allen, whom I had known when he was a police officer at Thomson's Falls. He was in charge of the hotel until the new owner, a Colonel Pink, arrived. Ba Allen took it upon himself to put us up. He had some beds arranged in a sort of cabin thatched with *makuti* leaves on the hotel roof, which was both airy and pleasant. Petley's was a two-storeyed building with magnificent teak staircases to the upper floors, whose extremely primitive sanitary arrangement provided a marked contrast. Dirty water flowed straight down onto the beach. The toilets on the first floor consisted of large pipes leading down into a ditch below— a form of sanitation known to generations of colonials as a "long-drop."

We were there just a few weeks before Independence, and the streets were still full of members of the Mau Mau exiled to

Lamu. They had been provided with a government pension sufficient to live reasonably and still send a good bit back to their families. They were obviously well-educated men, some of whom later played a part in running the country. They met in the evenings in Petley's bar, where they stood out from the rest of the population both by their physical appearance—they were Kikuyus—and by their ostentatious beards.

The locals eked out a meagre living from fishing and exporting mangroves, which were highly valued for construction work, to the Gulf. In spite of their limited means the people were hospitable and welcoming, as in most societies not yet contaminated by tourism.

The big two-masted dhows in the harbour, which came under sail from the Emirates, provided an animated spectacle with their constant coming and going. Sadly, they have nearly all disappeared now to be replaced by cargo ships and lorries. I believe Kenyatta suspected the dhow captains of smuggling all manner of contraband, and it was he who finally put an end to this picturesque thousand-year-old traffic.

On our return flight we saw another, larger herd of elephants. Onslow amused himself by flying very low so I could I film them. The elephants were not amused, and showed their anger by lifting their trunks high in the air in our direction. We had been allowed a glimpse of the Garden of Eden, a familiar sight in those days. The destruction of African fauna is not a myth, as my many memories and the films I have kept bear witness.

Two years later I returned to Lamu in my own plane with my father. We made for Petley's Inn, now the property of peppery Colonel Pink, who invited us to tea on the terrace. It was not just a courtesy but also a ruse to look us over and reassure himself that we were respectable enough to be put up in his hotel. We must have made the grade, as we were allowed to stay.

Father and I walked to Shella, a two-mile trek along the beach, impossible at high tide. It was exceedingly hot and humid, but some kind soul had put out benches, at long intervals, for weary travellers, for which we were most grateful. Shella was more or less in ruins, but on rounding a point, there at the beginning of the immense stretch of beach was a magnificent mansion built in authentic Swahili style. It belonged to Henry Burnier, a wealthy Swiss—related to the family who own Nestlé. Burnier was a convert to Islam and had become a learned and respected Muslim. He had made several pilgrimages to Mecca, and religious dignitaries came to consult him on matters touching on tradition and Koranic doctrines. In spite of being so well-liked and respected, however, he was forced to leave Lamu in 1966 at the time of the troubles with Somalia. He had a farm at Witu on the estuary of the Tana, and the Somalis objected to the presence of a European, no matter how devout a Muslim, and made threats on his life. As the government showed no great enthusiasm for protecting him, Burnier moved to Mombasa and ended his days as honorary consul for the Swiss Confederation.

His house, bought by the Danish Korschen family, became the Peponi, one of Kenya's finest hotels. This Italian-sounding name has nothing to do with Italy: it is a Swahili word meaning "place in the wind," or "paradise," and it is a fact that the moment one rounds the point leading to the hotel, one is conscious of the clean, fresh breeze from the ocean, a relief from the moist heat of the town. It is mainly because of this that the majority of Europeans chose to live at Shella, which is much cooler than the main town.

During the first few years of my coming to Lamu it was simply somewhere to get away to, and I never thought of buying a place there. As time went by, however, I became friendly with a number of interesting and intelligent people who had made Lamu their home, of whom Jim de Vere Allen was one. He was passionately interested in Swahili art, and taught me to love and appreciate it. He also founded the remarkable Lamu Museum, which he opened to preserve the treasures of the past for future generations. He moved heaven and earth to fund this project and was able to buy historic artefacts owned by local families who had no idea of their intrinsic value, but much to his credit he always paid good prices.

De Vere Allen was born in Kenya, where his father was the

deputy commissioner of prisons. His mother was a history professor. He had been educated in Uganda, had became a historian,
and had lived in Indonesia and studied Indonesian civilization.
He did much to prevent Lamu from becoming, like Zanzibar, a
shanty town and heap of ruins. He pushed the government into
buying up entire streets, which he rehabilitated, converting houses into flats for civil servants to rent. Once the rot had been
arrested, craftsmen took heart and once again began to make traditional furniture, and the wealthier inhabitants were sufficiently impressed to restore their houses, and to build new ones; even
the abandoned coral quarries on the island of Manda were
reopened and worked again.

George Fegan was an eminent vascular surgeon in Dublin and
London. He had perfected a revolutionary method for the treatment of varicose veins. At forty-nine he had a coronary and his
colleagues, realizing that unless he immediately changed his
lifestyle he would not survive for long, begged him to stop work
and rest. He decided to take their advice and to retire to Kenya.
One of his great interests was old paintings and he was a frequent visitor to Sotheby's in London. A lady on their staff who
knew George was soon leaving for Kenya asked whether he
would mind taking out a bottle of gin she had bought as a present for a friend out there.

"I promised I would send him one and I know he would be
delighted to receive it," she said, handing over the parcel. "His
name is Latham Leslie Moore, and he lives in Lamu."

Arriving at Nairobi airport Fegan took a taxi. As he was getting into the cab he said to the driver:

"Before taking me to the hotel, could we make a little detour
to Lamu. I have a parcel to deliver there."

"But, sir," said the bemused driver, "Lamu is over three hundred miles from here and it would take us at least two days to
get there"

"I see," replied George. "No matter. Let's go to the hotel." He
decided to keep the bottle for his own use, or at least until such
time as an opportunity presented to deliver it.

Some months later he was sitting on the terrace of the Castle Hotel Inn in Mombasa when he overheard some young travellers who, like himself, were passing through.

"I'd love to go to Lamu," said one, "but I haven't enough money left even for a bus ride."

To George, who still had the bottle of gin, the name of Lamu struck a chord.

"I'm quite keen to get to Lamu myself, but I'm not very well and couldn't carry my suitcase. If you will help me I'll cover your expenses."

"Done," said the delighted backpacker and George had found his man.

On reaching Lamu, George was transported with joy.

"I knew instantly that I had found my Nirvana, my Shangri-La, the one and only place in which I would find happiness."

George has lived at Shella ever since. He is now in perfect health, and every morning takes a walk along the beach—a little matter of a dozen miles or so. He has far surpassed Cadet Rousselle's (the hero of the French folksong) record of three houses: George must have built at least a dozen—he just likes building and furnishing houses. Delighted with each one he builds, he settles in and makes a garden. Soon he tires of it and starts to cast around for another "ideal" site, and having sold his present house, begins the whole cycle all over again. He can indulge his passion for moving house only because land prices and building costs are nothing like those in Europe. Nonetheless, Lamu's economy has benefited considerably from the arrival of men like de Vere Allen and Fegan, who are true conservationists and care deeply for the place.

Ba Allen was another picturesque character. The locals nick-named him "Bwana Kicheka" because of his booming laugh, which could be heard miles away. He affected to be a Muslim, went regularly to the mosque and took part in all the religious processions. He was also a notorious Don Juan, and it was said that he had a pretty charmer on every island of the archipelago. He went back to England from time to time and on one such visit he died in a senseless road accident, mown down by a trailer that had broken loose.

Ba's brother, Bunny Allen, was a famous white hunter. For years, long before shooting game was forbidden, Bunny took dozens of stars of stage and screen on safari. Today, aged eighty-six, he and his wife Jeri still live in Lamu, where he spends his time writing books. In 1973 Jeri Allen persuaded me to build a house of my own at Shella. She told me she had found an ideal site and that I should grab it before it was sold to someone else— Lamu was becoming a fashionable watering place and prices were rising as people began building holiday homes at Shella.

There were many good reasons for me to build at Shella. My work brought me more and more frequently to Lamu, although the long flight had originally put me off somewhat. Also, many of my friends lived at Shella—besides those I have already mentioned there were many others, such as the anthropologist Jean Brown, Pamela Scott, Richard and Annie Hughes, and the Leakeys, all interesting and stimulating people whose company gave me great pleasure. And, I had had enough of "perching" in other people's homes or having to stay at the Peponi.

Thrilled at the idea of a place of my own, I decided to take up Jeri Allen's offer. She was delighted at the thought of having me as a neighbour. I asked Jim Allen to be my architect and to draw up the plans for the house. We were anxious to reconstitute an authentic seventeenth-century Swahili house with a central courtyard, galleried first floor, and a *makuti*-roofed terrace on top. An important feature of the design was the inclusion of a characteristic Muslim *daka*, a little porch beside the front door opening directly onto the street, with stone benches for male guests not allowed into the house proper, traditionally the sanctuary of women.

The new medical program for Lamu district, for which I was responsible, offered the opportunity to help a region that fascinated me. It was even more important than providing work for the stonemasons and supporting traditional local craftsmen. In these remote areas there are primitive communities hidden away in the swamps and forests or tucked away on the island, some of them seeming hardly to have emerged from prehistoric times. Their way of life is at the mercy of floods and droughts, when they are not fleeing from one of the marauding armed bands of *shiftas* who periodically descend on them from Somalia.

Lamu, though constantly hyped in the glossy tourist magazines I see from time to time, is no tropical St. Tropez. Certainly it is a beautiful place: the sea is warm and the miles of beaches are almost empty. But sanitary conditions are deplorable. The water table is contaminated—the more's the pity, since there is no shortage of water. There is plenty of rain, which is filtered by the dunes, and there are wells everywhere—if only they were properly maintained and not, as happens quite often, used as latrines. The bad drains and the inefficient system of refuse collection leave filthy puddles and pools that breed malarial mosquitoes. So the package is exceedingly pretty but best not unwrapped. (I don't relish having to describe the down side of this paradise but, as a doctor, I feel I must.)

The first medical officer representing the ministry with whom I collaborated over this particular program was a tall, handsome Sikh, Dr. Panessar Singh, who turned the heads of all the young ladies in the area. A first-rate doctor and administrator, he did not spend his time holed up in his office and was always keen to fly with me on my rounds. He took the trouble to get to know his patients and their customs and habits, and he could always find someone to repair his boats, which was quite an achievement in Lamu. So far as I was concerned he had only one fault: I simply could not keep up with his long legs. It was not so much that he walked particularly fast, just that I had to take two strides to his one. One day as we were nearing Tchundwa I went on strike: I sat down on a stone and flatly refused to move.

"Just leave me here and go on alone. I just can't keep up with you."

Poor Singh was so contrite and apologetic—he had never realized what an effort it was for me to keep up with his giant strides.

To get the vaccination program off to a good start we went on a grand tour, stopping off wherever there was the smallest dispensary or health centre, doling out drugs and vaccines. In places where there were no such facilities we set up shop in the local school. The list of villages we had to service was as long as a litany: Mararani, Manda, Mangai, Ishakani, Mokokoni, Kiwayu, Fasa, Siyu, Pate...I know it by heart. In a few months we succeeded in covering the whole district. Later, when all the dispensaries were equipped with gas- or solar-powered refrigerators, they were able to organize their own vaccination program while we concentrated all our efforts on more remote communities with no medical facilities at all. The results of these visits have been very encouraging: Lamu district, not easy to cover completely, now has one of the best vaccination records in the whole country.

The people who live on the coast are more diverse in their origins and customs than the northern nomads or the agricultural population of central Kenya. Consequently their disease patterns are different. For example, the people of Kiunga are peasants who cultivate copra but are also fisherfolk, and they get a fairly well-balanced diet. There are sometimes cases of malnutrition among them but these are due in part to the fact that Muslim women do not breast-feed their babies for long.

In the hinterland, hidden in the depths of a dense forest dotted with copper-coloured baobab trees, are the Boni, who are hunter-gatherers living on flour made from dates and the berries of a bush that resembles the arbutus, or strawberry tree. Formerly they hunted elephant with their great bows and arrows but this is now forbidden—not that there are many elephants left to hunt. However, the place still teems with wildlife, and in particular with big antelopes resembling topi, which provide protein for the Boni.

On one occasion I was a guest of the Boni at Mangai for a circumcision ceremony. They were giving a great fiesta with dances and a sumptuous feast. Large platters heaped with crushed corn and succulent antelope steaks were placed on the ground. This technically illegal delicacy seemed to be much appreciated by one of the guests, a member of the local police who, like his superiors, knew there was no point in forbidding the Boni to hunt game since they had no other resources or means of survival. Also, no incriminating evidence, such as bows and arrows, was to be found in the Boni villages. They were so cunningly hidden up trees and in bushes that only those in the know could find them. I bought two of these bows for my watchmen, who knew exactly how to use them: the bow cost thirty shillings while the arrow cost sixty. This sounds strange, but apparently it is much simpler to make a bow than an arrow that will fly true.

At Witu, on the estuary of the Tana, the Orma and their animals live almost permanently in water. While the Boni are proto-Somalis, the Orma come from much farther away. They are related to the Galla of the northern deserts, speaking the same language, and one can only wonder how they ended up where they are. They live in attractive, elliptically shaped huts made of woven reeds and rushes, which are also used to make their beds and furniture. Their illnesses are linked to their aquatic environment. They are particularly prone to bilharzia, which is caused by tiny parasites penetrating the skin to reach the circulatory system, eventually settling in the intestines or bladder. Although bilharzia is not a life-threatening illness, it causes anemia and is extremely debilitating; it usually first shows itself by blood in the urine. Today drugs such as praziquantel and metrifonate are used with great success to treat it.

The diseases that are amenable to the classic vaccines such as DTP, BCG, polio, measles have become rare whereas malaria is still rampant. The population has acquired partial immunity, but from time to time severe malaria outbreaks flare up and it is children who bear the brunt. Another known parasitic disease is Bancroftian filariasis, also transmitted by mosquitoes, albeit of a different genus. This causes elephantiasis, a monstrous swelling of the legs or the scrotum. It affects mainly men, since Muslim women do not go into the fields. (This scandalizes the Kikuyu, who say they are lazy—Kikuyu women work in the field, so their men can go to the town.) There are also sometimes outbreaks of dengue, which used to be known to the British as "break-bone fever" because it can cause pain as severe as that of breaking a bone; this is caused by a mosquito-borne virus. It is important to check the blood in the early stages as the symptoms are similar to those of malaria, and while dengue has no specific treatment, malaria of course can be effectively treated, so wrong diagnosis could be fatal. High blood pressure with its consequent danger of stroke and paralysis, is common in the islands. I believe this hypertension is caused by too much salt in the staple diet of fish; the water too is brackish. Even the young are subject to circulatory troubles although, in general, Africans have low blood pressure. It is on record that when the Masai or Samburu are recruited into the army their blood pressure is low but as soon as they adopt the diet provided by army rations it rises.

Coastal women are wide of pelvis and give birth more easily than do up-country females and it is rare for them to need a caesarean section. On the other hand, the coastal mothers are prone to eclampsia, a serious complication of pregnancy manifested by alarmingly high blood pressure and convulsions, followed by coma. I was once called out to fetch a young girl from Siyu who was suffering from these symptoms. She was about fifteen years old and was six months pregnant with her first child. Eclampsia usually strikes in the middle three months of a first pregnancy. The diagnosis was clear and the prognosis grave, and as the hospital at Lamu was not equipped to treat such a case and I took her and her mother to Mombasa, where eight days later the patient died.

Six months later I returned to Siyu for a vaccination programme. To get to the clinic from the airstrip I had to pass through the village. In the middle of the street, a woman stopped me.

"Mama Daktari, I wanted to give you this to thank you," and she held out a little paper bag containing six eggs. I recognized the mother of the poor girl who had died of eclampsia.

"But why are you thanking me? I am so sorry that we were unable to save her."

"I know, but I wanted to thank you for trying."

I was deeply touched by this gesture. The value of the gift was not important. For these people eggs have a profound significance: they are given to young mothers as a symbol of life. I have never received a more splendid reward than those eggs given to me at Siyu.

George Fegan and I established and financed a small foundation to help paralysed youngsters. These boys had broken their spines in accidents and had neither insurance nor any help from social welfare. The most heart-breaking case was that of Abdullah, who was nineteen when he dived off a pontoon at Mombasa when the tide was out and the water too shallow. Since that time he has been paralysed from the neck down. His grandmother, who lives in Lamu, took him in and looks after him, and the trust gives her 500 shillings a month. Abdullah is a highly intelligent young man whose greatest passion is music and whose greatest joy is the cassettes we bring him. He is well aware of the disaster that has befallen him. What is so extraordinary is that he has survived for so long, for as a rule, people as crippled as Abdullah do not live long.

Few of the other patients are as severely disabled as Abdullah. Their injuries are due to a variety of accidents, such as falling from a coconut tree, or off a lorry. We try to give them the right aids—a walking frame, crutches and the like—and whenever possible we send them the physical education centre at Voi.

The little trust is our *harambee*—a Swahili word that, roughly translated, means "pulling together." Invented by Kenyatta, *Harambee* is a typically Kenyan idea that involves demanding "voluntary" contributions point-blank from tax-paying citizens to raise funds for and promote a number of enterprises, from bridges to hospitals to roads, all of which would be the responsibility of the state if the taxes were properly administered.

George Fegan, now happily installed in Lamu, had not forgotten the bottle of gin for Latham Leslie Moore and in due course he bought another bottle and delivered it in person. In this way he heard the life story of a most picturesque and extraordinary character, and heaven knows we have plenty of them in Kenya.

Latham came from a very good family. An only child, his parents had not bothered much with him, and he spent his childhood mostly in the company of grooms and gardeners who worked on the family estate. This neglect he attributed to the fact that he was one of the illegitimate children of Edward VII. This was no rumour: it was a fact, and the King had admitted paternity before his death. As an adult, Latham accentuated his undeniable resemblance to his natural father by wearing the familiar neatly trimmed, pointed beard.

Latham was prospecting for oil in the Antilles in 1914 when the First World War broke out. He joined up, and having risen to the rank of captain, he fought at the front in France, where he was badly gassed. When the war ended his doctors gave him only a short time to live. He travelled to Tanganyika, where the climate was supposed to be kinder to burnt-out lungs, and stayed there to carve out a career in agriculture until the 1940s.

It was when he retired that the legend of Latham really took off. Having heard that a small island called Msimbati was for sale, he decided that at all costs he must have it. His motivation was obscure but it is possible that he, the rejected, illegitimate son of a king, wanted to reign over his own kingdom. The island was situated south of Tanganyika, almost on the Mozambique border. Msimbati was to be auctioned on a certain date in a town close to the island. Latham decided to stay in the town before the auction was due to take place. He made it his business to meet the District Commissioner with whom, as a one-time civil servant himself, he had no difficulty making friends. He visited him daily at his place of work, and each time he did so, he surreptitiously moved the hand of the clock that dominated the office where the sale was to be held. At the end of the week nobody had noticed that the clock was an hour fast. At the appointed time, and what was thought to be the correct hour, the auctioneer opened the bidding for the island. Latham was the only bidder present and, just as he had planned, his bid was accepted, and he became the possessor of Msimbati. An hour later, on the dot, the other bidders for the island arrived only to find the auction was over and the doors of the sale-room closed.

Latham Leslie Moore reigned for a long time over his island, making it into an independent little sultanate and flying his own flag over his house. He was an experienced agriculturist, and under his regime the island and its inhabitants prospered. The government turned a blind eye to his activities until the fatal day when revolution broke out in Mozambique against the Portuguese colonists. Nyerere, who sympathized with the rebels, wanted Msimbati back as a discreet place in which to train freedom fighters. Determined not to lose his island, Latham publicized his plight to the whole world. This did not save him, however, and he was evicted by military *force majeure*.

The American journalist John Heminway and his friend Mary Anne Fitzgerald, who had often visited Latham on his island and had become fond of the eccentric old man, helped him take refuge in Lamu. Since it was also an island, they hoped he would not feel too strange or homesick there. He suffered from severe vitamin deficiency, and when I was in Lamu I used to give him a vitamin injection at 6:30 every morning. He walked with difficulty and in order to transport him from place to place, we rigged up a sort of sedan chair from bamboo poles lashed to an armchair, a pitiful conveyance for a deposed sovereign.

Latham lived off a small pension that made it possible for him to rent a house in the old Shella village. He had become very bitter, and quarrelled with his neighbours and friends. Eventually Heminway, various other friends and I decided that the climate was bad for Latham and that we should try to settle him somewhere more suitable, so we installed him in a hotel at Nanyuki in the Highlands. At first he seemed quite content, surrounded by tourists who were enchanted by his stories and anecdotes, but eventually however, he fell out with everyone and moved away. He ended up in the Nanyuki Cottage Hospital, where he died, having nearly made it to 100—not a bad life span for someone given a few years to live sixty-five years earlier.

During the forty-five years I have been practising medicine in Africa I have often been confronted with the awesome powers exercised by witch doctors, healers, herbalists and sorcerers of all kinds. We are in a continent where tradition, superstition and the supernatural form part of the infrastructure of society. It would have been stupid to ignore them and useless to try to fight them.

When I was making my debut as a bush doctor, I used to be annoyed when patients told me they were also going to a witch doctor. They hardly needed to tell me, for the cuts and burns on their skin from the magic rites told the story quite clearly. Putting on my intimidating Big Voice, I used to say, "You must choose between his methods or mine." But slowly it dawned on me that this was not the right way to obtain a patient's confidence. The witch doctor's treatment was mainly psychological in that he calmed and reassured the patient by saying he had appeased the spirit of his ancestors or the wicked genie who wished him harm. Overall, traditional healers in Kenya deal with the mind as well as the body. This strength has maintained their popularity, especially in situations where socio-economic and other cultural factors interfere with the use of modern health-care facilities.

I eventually came to the conclusion that my medicines were far more efficacious in treating bodily symptoms than the methods of the healer, but that the healer put the patient into a more relaxed state, which was beneficial for both the patient and my treatment. When an African is taken ill he thinks he is being punished because he has infringed a tribal taboo, or because an enemy has put an evil spell on him, and he tries to discover the cause of his illness—whom he has upset, what evil he has committed, or who may have a grudge against him. He goes off to consult the witch doctor, the *m'ganga*, who he believes will solve the problem and find a remedy, which may take a number of forms.

Accompanied by my friend the ethnologist Jean Brown, I went to see a famous *m'ganga*, Mweia wa Isopia. He practised his craft in the mountains of Kamba country and people flocked from far and wide to see him. While awaiting their turn, patients sat in on the preceding consultations, which took place in the open air. (This is also how I operate when I do my bush clinics.) The sick did not seem to mind the interest taken in their particular case by the audience—for Africans, illness is neither secret nor shameful.

The mighty Isopia made great play with bones and a variety of animal horns, and made his patient wave a hand over piles of shells. He then had him sit on a big, black, upended earthenware pot and made him lick black pastes. Next, he made him turn round, then he walked round the patient, had him stand up and crawled between his legs, finally becoming extremely agitated and rushing around in a frenzy. He drank a great deal of beer while doing all this and came out in a muck sweat. Half an hour later he pronounced his verdict: "You have offended such and such an ancestor of three or four generations ago. To calm him you will have to offer him a sacrifice." Then followed the prescription, specifically adapted to each case, which had to be carried out to the letter. For instance, he must kill a goat and offer a feast to a certain number of his friends. If the witch doctor thought his patient was the victim of an evil spell he gave him a vague description of the guilty person and of the place where he or she was to be found, and named a certain sum that had to be paid in order to remove the evil spell.

Isopia made a very good living and was said to earn more than a thousand shillings a day. I had the feeling that he deserved every penny of his fees, for he certainly worked hard for his money. If I had to get myself into such a lather for each and every patient under my care I would only have the time to see a very limited number of people. Patients came from Mombasa, Nairobi and Kisumu to consult him. Dozens of little bags hung from the roof of his hut, and he explained to me that they were charms.

"Those up there belonged to my grandfather, and the others over there to my father. But I am not allowed to use them, I had to make my own. When I die the son I have chosen to be my successor will also have to make his own charms and he will hang those I used from the rafters."

I bought an old calabash filled with black powder from Isopia. I have no idea what it was used for but my African staff are terrified of it.

A Masai sorceress called Seguenan lived near Magadi. She claimed her magical powers were the result of a sojourn at Tanga, a kind of training centre for magicians, healers and witch doctors, where she said she had spent a week in a cow's stomach, the cow being a sacred animal to the Masai. She was a handsome woman, tall and slim, with a powerful personality. She was wealthy, being the possessor of a great number of cows. The Masai said that when her herd went off to graze in the morning, the procession lasted for hours.

Seguenan welcomed all forms of progress and came to visit us at the stand we had taken at the Nairobi Show, where we were promoting our mobile health care. Her methods were similar to those practised by Chinese doctors. She charged families in her area a fee of two shillings per annum, in exchange for which she promised to do all she could to keep the community healthy. She was extremely intelligent and welcomed our mobile units when they arrived in Masailand. To show her goodwill she asked us to begin our visits in her village. She gave instructions that everyone should be vaccinated—an astute move since it was in her best interest to encourage anything that would keep her patients healthy. Naturally, she took all the credit for their continued good health but we felt that she had more than earned her fee.

Seguenan encouraged us in the belief that the ideal solution to African health problems would be a synergism between traditional and contemporary therapies. She had rapidly recognized the importance of preventive medicine, and whenever we arrived in Masailand she would come to our dispensaries, listen to our advice and take good note of our prescriptions and treatments.

It is undeniable that magic and superstition play important roles in regulating instant social justice. Armed with this knowledge I was able to settle, to satisfaction, a problem of domestic thefts at Ol Kalou. I had bought two cases of liquor at an auction. One contained Highland Mist, an excellent whisky, while the other held a special cognac. I had locked the precious bottles away in a cupboard but in spite of this precaution I noticed the levels going down at a great rate, and not long afterwards I found a cache of empty bottles hidden away in the high grass behind the kitchen. Although the labels had been removed the peculiarly shaped bottles were easily recognizable.

I suspected my old cook, who was an excellent cook but very fond of strong drink. Having no proof, there was no way I could accuse him outright, and anyway I did not want to lose him. I was less worried about the pilfering of my cellar than about the effect such large quantities of alcohol would have on the old man's liver. I knew if he went on drinking at his present rate he would not last very long.

I decided to go for broke using traditional methods. One of the guards at Thomson's Falls Co-operative Society had been recommended to me as a part-time *m'ganga*. He was a Luo, a very dignified personage in his fine uniform. I gave him a detailed report of my problem, whereupon he asked whom I suspected and then asked me to drive him to the village.

"From there I will make my own way to your farm. On my walk I will meet with and chat to various people who will provide me with information."

When he reached the farm he asked that all fifteen members of my staff should assemble under the big olive trees that grew close to the house. He opened the session with a prayer. Then he asked the youngest member of the staff, a lad who looked after the horses, to hold a little box containing a black paste for him. From it he took an ordinary sewing needle and having chanted some incantations he spoke in solemn tones.

"There have been many thefts here. We shall soon know the guilty ones. They must return that which they have stolen, or terrible things will happen to them."

He then ordered those present to put out their tongues and not to put them in again. The general effect of this instruction was extremely comical, but nobody seemed inclined to laugh. Then, using a spatula the witch doctor smeared a little of the black paste onto each tongue and stuck the needle into the paste. Each time, until he reached the cook, the needle wobbled and fell over, but when he stuck it into the cook's tongue it remained firmly fixed.

"So you are the culprit," cried the *m'ganga*. "You will now tell us what you stole. Was it money, wine, food, alcohol or clothing?"

With his tongue hanging out with a needle in it the suspect

could not speak. So he nodded, or shook his head in answer to the questions put to him. Though dumb, he made a complete confession of guilt.

The witch doctor pronounced sentence: "You must pay for the bottles you stole. The money will be stopped out of your wages, and you will pay me fifty shillings a month for six months."

At this juncture I called a halt to the consultation, for I did not think it fair that the cook should be responsible for the whole payment to the *m'ganga*. I insisted that half the sum should be paid by the whole staff to the witch doctor, while I would pay the other half. In this way justice was seen to be done, everyone was associated with the affair and, as was my intention, complete trust was restored all round. Once the bargain had been struck, the witch doctor made a sign, and the needle, still upright in the cook's tongue, fell off, although the cook and the *m'ganga* were standing 10 feet apart.

I was sure it was a trick, but so far nobody has been able to give me a rational explanation of this curious happening. What is even stranger is that the sorcerer used his needle trick on several other employees known to have pilfered food or clothes, which was not a great crime, being considered as staff "perks." Just how did the *m'ganga* pinpoint the culprits?—I had only pointed him in the direction of the cook. Without disputing his gifts as a soothsayer I imagined he had gathered a great deal of useful inside information in his preliminary investigation during his walk to the farm. The very next day after this little domestic drama had taken place, spades, shovels and all manner of gardening implements that had gone missing reappeared in the gardening shed as if by magic.

As for the cook, there was, of course, no question of his reimbursing me for the full value of all the alcohol he had imbibed, but I was pretty certain he had learned his lesson and would cut down on his consumption of drink. I had a great regard for my cook, a Kipsigis, who had sacrificed himself to give his children as good an education as possible. One of them, in fact, became a general.

At Loliondo Dr. Wachinger, an Austrian medical missionary, spent years combating the powerful influence of a *Laibon*, a

Masai witch doctor who obstinately refused to allow European doctors to work in his territory and did all he could to obstruct them. Eventually this intractable individual developed cancer and decided to have an operation in the local hospital. He survived the operation for some time, but when he died, the Masai realized very quickly that the implacable enemy of Western medicine had finally laid down his arms. Such cases of volte-face are more and more frequent. Even those with strong reservations know now that, though we cannot perform miracles, they have to admit defeat and join our camp. One of our greatest victories had been to stop fighting the practitioners of traditional African medicine and instead make them our allies. We never try to prevent any patient from visiting a *m'ganga*, but, in exchange, we ask the *m'gangas* to send us the seriously ill patients they are unable to treat.

This may sound like a Utopian dream but in practice it works. We teach our African colleagues how to detect anemia caused by malnutrition so that they can, on their own, prescribe a more varied and healthy diet for example, iron-rich vegetables for nursing mothers who have had a hemorrhage. We have convinced them to encourage vaccination, thus halting epidemics. It has been a slow process but I think it is fair to say that the Africans have come round to accepting our ways of treating the sick. Today, women who refuse to have their children vaccinated are strongly criticized by other members of their community.

In areas sparsely covered by medical care we could not ban traditional midwives who had no knowledge of asepsis in childbirth. We went along with their methods, but were careful to provide them with simple but effective ways of combating their lack of hygiene. We gave them matchboxes containing a small piece of antiseptic soap to wash their hands with and we issued them with a new razor blade to cut the umbilical cord and twists of thread to tie it. These modest aids, meant to be used for one labour only and then thrown away, were the best and most inexpensive forms of defence we could provide for the prevention of countless cases of postnatal tetanus and puerperal sepsis.

I cannot pretend that everything is rosy in the world of the

African witch doctor. The *m'ganga* is generally a good medicine man, but there is also his opposite, the *m'chawi*—the wicked one to whom one has recourse if one wishes to take revenge on an enemy or to eliminate a rival. The *m'chawi* can bewitch people or, worse still, supply poisonous draughts. To make matters more complicated, the *m'ganga* and the *m'chawi* can also be one and the same person, who takes on whichever role meets the occasion.

One day a man was brought to my surgery at Ol Kalou. He was in a cataleptic state, rigid and ice-cold. He was unconscious, but his pulse was normal. I tried by every means in my power to bring him round but without success. The place was abuzz with rumours that he had been bewitched. I sent him to the hospital at Nakuru where he was thoroughly examined and investigated but no trace of meningitis or other infection or virus could be found. He did not seem to be suffering from any known symptoms, yet, in spite of being given intravenous fluids, the man died eight days later without having regained consciousness, theoretically in perfect health. I heard later that there had been a feud in his clan and that he might have been poisoned.

Witch doctors are extremely knowledgeable when it comes to poisons. While carrying out an autopsy I have sometimes come across strange seeds mixed with the food in the deceased's stomach. Certain bushes are known to produce a substance very similar to curare that can paralyse, and ouabain, used to smear on the barbs of poisoned arrows, was once used in cardiology.

We have much to learn from Africans about medicinal plants, which is another reason for us to collaborate with their traditional herbalists. We should not forget that the majority of medicines in the Western pharmacopoeia originate from plant sources—for example, aspirin from the willow and quinine from Cinchona bark. When visiting the Pokot I used to attend consultations of a female *m'ganga*. She did not practise magic but was a healer, using medicinal herbs and plants. I used to buy samples of the potions she prescribed to try them out. At Sigor, in the rainy season when there is a malaria scare the inhabitants boil a certain bark and pour the liquid into a big calabash, and every morning the villagers drink a cupful as a preventive measure. I tried some of the infusion and it tasted of quinine.

I do not make use of herbal medicines in my work, but I am fully aware of their value as preventive medicine in the poorer regions of the African continent where the people cannot afford to buy sophisticated and expensive modern drugs. One day perhaps they may be able to do so, but in the meantime we must explore other paths and make use of the oldest and most effective herbal medicines, which for centuries have helped suffering Africans.

Traditions in Africa can be dangerous—for instance, the wounds made by ritual scarifications, circumcisions and excisions. It is difficult for me to overcome my revulsion at the custom of female circumcision, an atrocious mutilation of young girls from certain tribes that is and will remain the subject of lengthy and complex arguments. But without pronouncing any moral judgments on these tribal customs let us discuss only their medical aspect.

These practices offer an open door to infection, but today the danger to life has taken on an even wider and more urgent dimension. This is because of the terrible menace of AIDS, of which the Africans are becoming more and more aware. Because of the fear of AIDS, certain tribal customs now hang in the balance. More and more families have replaced female circumcision with merely symbolic ceremony. They still have their boys circumcised, but the operation now takes place in a clinic where the parents can be sure of antiseptic conditions.

Male circumcision is mandatory for all Kenyan tribes with the exception of the Luo and the Turkana. My Kikuyu friend Rosemary was not too strict about obeying tribal customs and did not have her two sons circumcised. But when the thirteen-year-old went to secondary school he was teased and mocked by his fellow pupils, so to save his feelings Rosemary felt obliged to send her boys to Nazareth Hospital at Limuru, where for the sum of 150 shillings, the thirteen-year-old and his seven-year-old brother were relieved of their foreskins and their worries.

African tribal customs are not to be trifled with. It is wiser not to try to tackle them head-on with our good old heavy-handed

Western logic. Members of one well-intentioned humanitarian organization working in Africa were upset by the way Ethiopian women went to work in the fields with their babies strapped to their backs, and the sight of infants' heads lolling about spurred the do-gooders to offer the mothers cradles. This gift was a disaster: tucked up in their cradles under shady trees, the infants were snatched by leopards, hyenas or monkeys. If they were left alone in the family hut, many perished when, as happens quite often, the thatched village huts caught fire. Eventually it became crystal clear that the only way of ensuring the safety of the infants was to follow the old, tried and tested traditional method that Ethiopian mothers had used for centuries: once more they carried their infants strapped to their backs, regardless of lolling heads .

On the other hand, simple modern measures such as the pieces of antiseptic soap in matchboxes that we gave to midwives have had spectacular success. We also obtained remarkable results from another ordinary but effective aid in the prevention of trachoma. All that was required was an empty tin.

Trachoma is a form of infectious conjunctivitis caused by poor hygiene, and a major cause of blindness in the Third World. The treatment is simple but vital: the eyes must be kept clean by regular bathing to prevent the infection being spread by flies or dirt. Since wells may be six or seven miles away or more, understandably nomads do not consider a long trek to fetch water from the well merely to wash their children's eyes a number one priority. We have taught the mothers to use the tins we give them. A small hole is pierced in the base of the tin, which is then fitted with a plug. The tin is filled with water and when the plug is removed, a tiny jet of clear water, sufficient to wash the children's eyes clean, comes out. The mothers are happy to use this simple but effective method of fighting trachoma, which has the added bonus of using only minute quantities of water.

One of our major battles, and one that simply must be won, is to persuade Africans to use condoms, the main weapon against the spread of AIDS. Many Africans refuse to believe the ravages AIDS has brought to their country. They say that the humanitarian organizations inflate statistics in order to obtain larger subsidies, though we who work in this particular field know only too well at first hand just how rapidly this fatal disease is spreading.

Five years ago we were asked to make a study of an epidemic that had hit the inhabitants of the remote valley of the Suguta, south of Lake Turkana. It is a dried-up piece of the lake, from which it was separated by a volcanic eruption, and it would be difficult to imagine a more inhospitable, inaccessible, scorching hot, lava-strewn place; yet people do live there. Dr. Philip Rees and his team established that the mounting death rate was caused by kala-azar, a parasite that attacks the spleen and lymph system and is transmitted by a sandfly that makes its home in anthills.

At first sight it seemed there was nothing exceptional about this epidemic, until blood samples taken from one of the men were analyzed: he was found to be HIV-positive. How on earth, the doctors asked, had this fellow, who lived at the end of the world, become infected? Today we all know of similar cases in our midst. One of my staff lost her aunt, who took a job as a waitress in a café catering to lorry drivers; she was dead in six months with AIDS.

At AMREF we have already lost three of our colleagues, and one of my friends, a young European, working as a safari guide, died of AIDS two years after being given a blood transfusion in Dar es Salaam after a motorcycle accident. We all know of dozens of similar examples and have no option but to believe in the terrifying statistics that are published.

In Kenya there is a very reliable system for obtaining statistics. Blood donors are not targeted, and do not form part of the groups at risk. They represent a middle-of-the-road section of the population. The HIV test that is regularly carried out on donors shows that 8 to 10 percent in the towns are HIV-positive, and 1 to 3 percent in the country. Infected blood is destroyed, but the blood donors are not told the results. Many other countries do the same but I wonder whether this procedure should not be a subject for discussion?

Recently at Subukia a man died of AIDS and from then on his

wife and family were ostracized. The Catholic priest remonstrat-
ed with his flock: "This unhappy woman has lost everything. She
is without any kind of resources. How can you abandon her in
this heartless fashion?" The faithful glumly parted with tiny
sums, but nobody went to see the widow. People are terrified of
AIDS and we have had to organize numerous meetings to reassure them and to give them factual information about AIDS, to
explain that this illness can only be transmitted through blood or
sexual relations. Their obsessive fear inhibits people from having
tests. They are frightened of being told the worst and of being
ostracized in their turn. AIDS is destroying the very basis of
African society—beginning with the solidarity that existed before
misfortune struck, when people helped one another through the
bad days.

AIDS mainly strikes down young, educated and active men
who form the vital force of their country. Since their sexual
habits are relatively loose, young males enjoy the favours of as
many females as they can while their spouses stay at home in
town or on the farm. This sexual freedom applies to all men,
whether farmers, civil servants or businessmen.

In Nairobi there are crowds of working women who, though
not professional prostitutes by any means, are willing to turn a
trick sometimes in order to stretch out their meagre incomes.
Neither they nor their partners can be bothered to use condoms—
"It's like eating sweets without removing their wrappers."

From time immemorial, policemen and soldiers who travel
extensively without their wives have been carriers of sexually
transmitted diseases. I don't have to be a Sherlock Holmes to
understand why I find cases of AIDS in remote parts of the desert
that are near to a garrison or frontier posts. The greatest danger
in East Africa comes from transport drivers who practise unpro-
tected sex. We have made a tremendous effort to make them
aware of their responsibility through a program of information
and education to teach them and their partners about sexually
transmitted diseases (particularly AIDS), and how to avoid them.
Drivers on the Malawi to Dar es Salaam run, for example, may
have ten to fifteen sexual encounters along the way. We want to

make these knights of the road aware of the risks they and their partners are running by ignoring the use of preventives.

I have known of a number of alarming cases such as that of a Rendille from Korr who, having infected his wife, who died, took a second spouse whom he duly infected with the result that she miscarried and lost her baby. At Subukia, I took charge of a young boy, the eldest of seven orphans whose father, a lorry driver, had died of AIDS. Their mother had died two years later. My protégé had attended a Catholic school. We got him a bursary that enabled him to continue his education at a college in Nakuru, where he is studying accountancy. But how many sad, solitary children and old people are left alone without support in the deserted villages and fallow soil of Uganda and Zaire? Far, far too many, even if one refuses to believe the statistics.

Our educational program is offered to lorry drivers who travel between Mombasa and Nairobi, and includes meetings, seminars, posters, brochures, cartoons, films and even songs and sketches. Similar resources are available at all the main stopping places used by the long-distance lorry drivers, and free condoms are available from dlspensers.

With the co-operation of the KAS (Know AIDS Society), AMREF has developed a campaign to combat the social and economic ravages caused by AIDS. This campaign is targeted at individuals, families and communities in the Nairobi area and includes health education, counselling and help for those stricken with the disease, and for their families and orphans. A similar program has been initiated in Tanzania on the road from Dar es Salaam to Mbeya in the Mwanza area. Lorry drivers are, at long last, becoming aware of the high rate of mortality from AIDS among their friends and the dangers of casual sex without preventives.

Kenya's other scourge, even more deadly than AIDS, is road accidents. Many could be averted if there was the will to take more positive action. Their incidence is far too high. Hardly a day passes without a child arriving at school with the news that a member of her family—father, brother or uncle—has been the victim of a road accident. The main cause of these accidents is the *matatu*, an ancient, rickety, heavily overladen "minibus" used as a collective taxi. These vehicles dart along at insane speeds taking passengers to their respective destinations, though very often they end up instead in a cemetery or in hospital. The owner of the *matatu* fleets are only interested in making money. They allow the vehicles to be driven into the ground, and have absolutely no regard for human life. The drivers, who double as fare-collectors and postmasters, are paid from their takings, and, equally, have no interest in the maintenance or safety of their vehicles as long as they run. To keep going they stuff themselves with *mirra*, a sort of marijuana, a natural amphetamine that makes them lose all sense of danger. When the *matatus* started, passengers paid three ten-cent coins to be transported in these coffins on wheels—hence their name. Today the fare is much higher, but any fare is too much if the destination is a mortuary.

It is difficult to change the manic way *matatu* drivers drive. Many of the vehicles belong to rich and influential people who themselves would certainly never travel in these vehicles; they drive in well-maintained luxury cars. According to the people of Nairobi, the *matatu* owners belong to the tribe of the Wa-Benzi—Mercedes-Benz owners.

Matatus apart, the incidence of fatal motor accidents is appallingly high. Cars go over cliffs or off the road because of badly signposted roadworks; drivers overtake through clouds of dust, or at the brow of a hill, and run head-on into a bus coming the other way. The police say nothing: a hundred shillings settles everything. In this particular domain collective responsibility has yet to be born.

More than half the cases we airlift are victims of road accidents. We do not operate an emergency treatment service, but we do transport the injured to the hospitals that can give them the best care. This service takes up a great deal of our time and equipment. The traditional stretcher proved unsuitable for use in a plane but thanks to a benefactor in France we have been able to make use of special transport shells manufactured to our own design for use in planes.

Sir Michael Wood died in Nairobi on 15 May 1987, of cancer of the kidney. He passed away at his home at Karen, west of Nairobi. It was here that he and Susan retired at the end of the seventies, having been forced to abandon their beloved farm at Kilimanjaro, into which they had poured so many years of love and effort, after it was expropriated as part of a Tanzanian policy of land redistribution.

Mike, as he was known to us all, had stood down from his post as director general of AMREF two years earlier, when he reached sixty-five, since he felt that he would now be safely leaving a thriving organization, able to function without him. He had created a new foundation, FARM (Food and Agricultural Research Management), to teach Africans more productive agricultural methods. In setting up this program he remained true to his early convictions: one must not just treat problems but rather their root causes when they involve poor husbandry and use of natural resources. Mike's old friend, the great South African writer Laurens Van der Post, emphasized this in his memorial tribute, which enshrined all Mike's theories.

"Michael was not only a surgeon. He was a healer both in the medical and social sense of the word. He had come to know Africa and to understand her people as few have done."

In the last few years the combination of the drought and the demands of refugees seeking asylum has made the work of humanitarian organizations more and more difficult, particularly as the rest of the world seems to be totally uninterested in the fate of the African continent. The same old clichés are once again bandied about—"Helping Africa is akin to Sisyphus hopelessly pushing his rock uphill or to the sieve-like cask of the Danaïdes," or, more recently, "The Africans are dying of starvation in front of a chest full of natural riches to which the key has been lost."

I agree about the chest: Africa is overflowing with great natural resources that are poorly exploited or sold far too cheaply on the world markets. So far, nobody seems to have taken account of the extraordinary talents of the African people, who are inventive, resourceful and great improvisers when the need arises, and who, more perhaps than any other people, are firm believers in solidarity. As for finding the key that opens the treasure chest, I think it is the West that might have confiscated it.

I wonder whether the Judaeo-Christian tradition did not invent hell in order to prove its own existence, as a negative of its own world that might help it to bear its own difficult reality? For a long time the communist countries played this role until, to everyone's great discomfort, they quit the scene. I wonder whether Africa is not being marked down to take their place? The West continues to blacken the name of the African continent to which they feel they have given so much and from which they now expect no return. It is a fine hell, the obverse of what passes for Paradise. Thus do we absolve ourselves, certain in the knowledge that we did well by Africa, we who colonized it so badly and decolonized it even worse fashion.

Europeans concentrate on East European problems because they are "nearer home." Africa is far, far away; the tribes are constantly warring with each other, and their rulers are corrupt and incompetent. But is this so different from what is happening in Eastern Europe, where factions attack each other on the pretext of "ethnic cleansing," yet they do not even have the excuse of not having known other models of social behaviour. In what way are the ex-dictators of the communist empire closer to us than the African leaders? And why should their struggle for liberty and justice for their people touch us more than that of the African crowds who courageously face a hail of bullets. Is it because the Eastern Europeans are white?

It is wishful thinking to pretend that Africa is too far away when it takes only a few hours by plane for the desperate and dispossessed seeking sanctuary in one of the rich and prosperous countries of Europe. Not that Africans want to leave their beloved country. They are never happy away from their native land, and leave only under duress, and when there is no other choice for survival. Yet come they will unless immediate measures are taken to help them to remain in Africa.

In northern countries, where immigration is an obsession, the notion of the population explosion in Africa is terrifying. A 1992 United Nations report states that today's world population, estimated at 5.5 billion, will reach 8.25 billion in 2025, and 10 billion in 2050, which means that within sixty years it will have doubled. In this time Africa will have tripled its population and will contain one-third of the world's population. If nothing is done to limit this explosion, the consequences for the natural resources of the country will be devastating, particularly when one remembers that today, at this very moment, more than one billion human beings are living in abject poverty. Nearly as many are illiterate, without access to potable water or to any kind of health or medical care. The birth rate in Africa is 43 per 1,000, compared to only 27 per 1,000 in Asia and Latin America, 14 per 1,000 in the United States and 13 per 1,000 in Europe. It is clear that only by careful family planning can the birth rate *and* the infant mortality rate be brought down. This is not a paradox. Having fewer children means they can be brought up under better living conditions, which means that in time they will also be better nourished and healthier.

This is the message we try to put across at our clinics. But efficient family planning needs better education for women, who at present are discriminated against in three-quarters of the world—two-thirds of the world's illiterate are women. Giving them an education and social status is the only way to prevent the catastrophic and ever-rising population explosion that threatens humanity.

Yet the world continues to turn on its axis. In the course of history few grand prophecies have been fully realized. One remembers the dire prophecies made by the Club of Rome in the seventies, many of which never came to fruition. For fifty years we have laboured under the belief that one half of the world would hurl itself on the other half, ending in a nuclear apocalypse. For decades the Soviets waited for American warplanes to rain bombs on their cities, and then the planes did arrive—instead of carrying death-dealing missiles, they came with supplies of food and medicine.

Long-term forecasts are nearly always wrong. In any case, if the future was flashed up on the screen there would only be resigned despair. The future is made up of what we start to build from today and what we will not tolerate for tomorrow. There is always time to act, and right now it is of vital importance to do so. That is what we at AMREF are doing.

In thirty-five years, our resources and goals have grown considerably, and the enthusiasm that motivated us in the beginning remains intact. We have not slackened our pace. I have lived long enough to know that the world follows fashions that soon become out of date and unfashionable. Fashions are as changeable as the African climate: Sometimes it is favourable, sometimes hostile, subject to forces that we know exist but that we have not yet managed to master.

I have never married or founded a family. Frankly, I have never had the time, and it is probable that marriage would not have suited my character. Also, what kind of man would have followed me in my peregrinations? In any case, my brother and sisters have made a sizable contribution to the growth of the French population, so the family honour is saved.

I may not have had any biological babies but I have many children—all those I have helped to survive and grow up and who still welcome me to their villages with glad cries of "Mama Daktari." In Swahili "Mama" means Madam; it also means mother, and in my heart this is what it means to me.

I have seen Africa at its best and at its worst. I have known it in joy and in sorrow. These last few years have been dire, but I believe that the best is yet to come, and that come it will.

AMREF
AROUND THE WORLD

Founders
The late Sir Arcibald McIndoe
Dr. Thomas D. Rees
The late Sir Michael Wood

AMREF Headquarters
P.O. Box 31025
Nairobi, Kenya
Tel: +254 2 501 301
Fax: + 254 2 506 112

AMREF Austria
A-5232 Kirchberg 27
Austria
Tel: + 43 77 47/52 42
Fax: + 43 77 47/52 42 5

AMREF Canada
59 Front St. East
Toronto, ON M5E 1B3
Tel: (416) 601-6981
Fax: (416) 601-6984

AMREF Denmark
12 H.C. Andersens Boulevard
DKD-1553
Kobenhavn V., Denmark
Tel: + 45 33 15 75 33
Fax: + 45 33 15 68 02

AMREF Germany
Mauerkirchenstr 155
D-81925 München 81
Germany
Tel: + 49 89 9811129
Fax: + 49 89 981189

AMREF France
c/o Mme D. Gautheron
66 Bis Rue St. Didier
75116 Paris, France
Tel: + 33 1 45538684
Fax: + 33 1 45532729

AMREF Italy
Piazza dei Martiri di Belfiore 4
00195 Rome, Italy
Tel: + 39 6 320 22 22/26
Fax: + 39 6 320 22 27

AMREF – The Netherlands
Jan van Brakelplantsoen 5
2253 TD Voorschoten
The Netherlands
Tel: + 31 71 762480
Fax: + 31 71 763777
Patron: HRH Prince Bernhard

AMREF South Africa
P.O. Box 11489
Pretoria 0001
South Africa
Tel: + 12 323 2079
Fax: + 12 323 2338

AMREF Sweden
103 75 Stockholm
Sweden
Tel: + 46 8 788 50 01
Fax: + 46 8 788 50 10

AMREF Tanzania
Upanga Road,
P.O. Box 2773
Dar es Salaam
Tel: + 255 51 46785
Fax: + 255 51 46440

AMREF Uganda
Plot 17
Nakasero Road,
P.O. Box 10663
Kampala, Uganda
Tel: + 256 41 250319
Fax: + 256 41 244565

AMREF UK
11 Old Queen Street
London, UK
Tel: + 171 233 0066
Fax: + 171 233 0099
Patron: HRH The Prince
   of Wales

AMREF USA
19 West 44th Street, # 1708
New York, NY 10036
Tel: (212) 768-2440
Fax: (212) 768-4230